European History

1000 Interesting Facts About Europe

Welcome Aboard, Check Out This Limited-Time Free Bonus!

Ahoy, reader! Welcome to the Ahoy Publications family, and thanks for snagging a copy of this book! Since you've chosen to join us on this journey, we'd like to offer you something special.

Check out the link below for a FREE e-book filled with delightful facts about American History.

But that's not all - you'll also have access to our exclusive email list with even more free e-books and insider knowledge. Well, what are ye waiting for? Click the link below to join and set sail toward exciting adventures in American History.

Access your bonus here: https://ahoypublications.com/

Or, Scan the QR code!

Table of Contents

Introduction

The history of Europe is full of incredible stories and complex developments. Each period has uniquely shaped the European continent, from the Upper Paleolithic period to the fall of the Berlin Wall. **This book provides insights into this vast and varied history by exploring dozens of key events that have affected Europe.**

We begin with a look at life in **western Eurasia during the Upper Paleolithic period,** some forty thousand years ago. **Explore how human society developed over thousands of years** and how agricultural practices were first introduced during the Neolithic Revolution.

Next, we take a closer look at **ancient Greece's impressive Minoan civilization,** which was later followed by **the Mycenaean civilization.** Explore interesting facts about **the Roman Republic and the Greco-Persian War.** Discover more information about **Charlemagne's coronation** in 800 CE and **the Viking invasions** that kicked off in 790.

Gain insight into how modern-day Europe was shaped through crucial revolutions and conflicts like **the French Revolution** and **the Napoleonic Wars.**

The book concludes by exploring some of the most significant European events during modern history, including World War I and II, the Cold War, and the Greek War of Independence, just to name a few.

Get ready to journey back through time and discover the incredible **history of Europe!**

Upper Paleolithic Period
(40,000–8000 BCE)

Unravel the secrets of the last part of the Stone Age with this section. Learn twenty intriguing **facts about how people lived during this period.** Did they use fire? Did they believe in gods? Did they leave any kind of records? Let's discover the answers to these questions!

1. **The Upper Paleolithic period was the last part of the Stone Age.** It began about forty thousand years ago in Europe.

2. **During this period, people lived in hunter-gatherer societies and made tools from stone,** which they used to hunt animals like mammoths, bison, and deer.

3. **People began using fire during this period to cook food,** keep warm in cold climates, and have a form of light at night.

4. **People started creating art by painting on cave walls** and carving sculptures out of bone or ivory.

5. **Over six hundred wall paintings adorn Lascaux, a cave complex in France.** It is debated how old these paintings are, but most archaeologists agree they are around seventeen thousand years old.

6. **Archaeologists have discovered several village sites across Europe** dating back to between 18,500 and 8000 BCE.

7. In parts of **Europe, such as France and Spain, there was a culture called the Solutrean,** which lasted from around 22,000 to 17,500 BCE.

8. **The technology used by the Solutrean included spears** with sharpened points made from bones that could be thrown over long distances.

9. **The name comes from the Solutré region of France,** where the earliest remains of weapon heads of that technology were found.

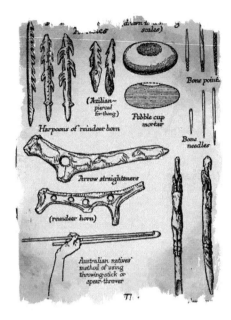

10. Another group known as **the Gravettians flourished in central Europe between 28,000 and 22,000 BCE.** These people were hunters who used horses to hunt wild animals, such as reindeer.

11. **The Gravettian culture is well known for its tools,** such as the Gravette points, which were used to hunt large animals.

12. **In some parts of Europe, people began burying their dead in tombs or graves** with offerings like jewelry and food. This was a sign they had developed spiritual beliefs.

13. **People began trading with other cultures during this period.**

14. **There was an increase in population size as people traveled farther away from their homes** in search of new resources.

15. **Clothing worn during the Upper Paleolithic included fur and leather garments.** People also wore jewelry made from animal bones or shells.

16. **Pottery would not become popular until much later.** At this time, most humans prepared food on open flames.

17. **While there is evidence that humans from the Upper Paleolithic era spoke different languages,** it is unclear whether or not these languages were related to the larger proto-Indo-European language group from which later European languages would develop.

18. **In what is now modern-day Russia and Ukraine, people cultivated wild grains** like rye and wheat, which allowed them to produce their food rather than relying entirely on hunting and gathering.

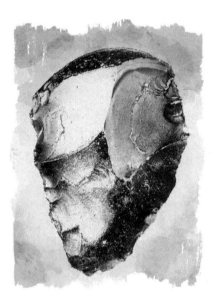

19. Toward the end of **the Upper Paleolithic Era** (around 12,000 BCE), some parts of **Europe experienced colder temperatures,** which limited the available resources like plants, animals, and water sources.

20. **Humans were forced to adopt a more settled lifestyle.** Farming became more common than hunting and gathering, but this process was accelerated during the Neolithic Revolution.

Mesolithic Period and Neolithic Revolution
(8000—4500 BCE)

Explore **twenty interesting facts about daily life during the Mesolithic period and the Neolithic Revolution.** We'll take a look at how people lived during these eras, from their homes to what they ate.

21. **Archaeologists call it the Mesolithic period, which means "Middle" Stone Age.** The Mesolithic period was between the Paleolithic (Old Stone Age) and Neolithic (New Stone Age) periods.

22. During this period, **people made their homes from materials like animal skins, reeds, branches, and clay** mixed with water to form walls that would keep out the wind and rain.

23. **Fishing was an important source of protein for many communities in Europe.** Some people had special boats that allowed them to fish more easily over larger areas of water.

24. **The Neolithic Revolution began around ten thousand years ago.** People started growing crops and keeping animals for food rather than relying solely on hunting and gathering.

25. **This period saw the emergence of the first permanent settlements in Europe,** as well as large-scale farming practices, which led to an increase in population density throughout regions like Britain and northern France.

26. **The Neolithic Revolution brought different advancements in technology,** such as the advent of polished axes in Europe. These tools could be used for chopping wood and cutting down trees faster than ever before.

27. **As populations increased, so did trade.** Goods could be exchanged between different areas and groups for things that weren't available locally, like metal and other raw materials.

28. By 4500 BCE (the end of this era), **societies had become much more complex.** Different social classes emerged due to increased wealth from trading or through military conquest.

29. **Ceramics were first produced during this period.** Pottery vessels served decorative and practical purposes in the home.

30. **The combination of farming and animal husbandry led to surplus yields,** which needed to be stored in newly developed granaries in order to preserve them for a long time.

31. **Religion became an important part of life.** It is believed that many religious ceremonies started taking place around this time in European history.

32. **Cattle were one type of livestock kept by people living in Europe at this time.** Cattle were valuable sources of protein, and their skins could be used for practical purposes.

33. **Archeological evidence suggests developments in the practice of herbalism – the use of plants as forms of medicine – during this period,** though such practices had emerged thousands of years earlier.

34. **It is believed the Neolithic Revolution spread to Europe from the Fertile Crescent in Mesopotamia,** where these developments occurred a couple thousand years prior.

35. **This meant that prominent crops from Southwest Asia were also introduced to Europe during this time, like barley and emmer.**

36. **The Neolithic Revolution saw the rise of monuments and towering stone structures called megaliths,** which were used as places for rituals, celebrations, or burials.

37. **Among the most well-known Neolithic megaliths in Europe are the Stonehenge in England and the Carnac Stones in northwestern France.**

38. **Artistic expression flourished during the Mesolithic period.** Cave paintings depicting animals or scenes from everyday life were created across Europe using natural pigments, such as red ochre.

39. **The domestication of sheep and goats for their wool and milk greatly impacted Europe's development during this era.** These animals provided food and materials from which to make clothing, which was important in cold climates.

40. **It is believed that women played important roles in their communities by gathering food, caring for children,** managing household tasks, and even participating in religious ceremonies alongside men.

Bronze Age
(3500–1200 BCE)

The Bronze Age in Europe was a remarkable time of innovation and growth. Tools and weapons were made from bronze for the first time, leading to increased mobility and trade. In this chapter, we will explore twenty interesting facts about the Bronze Age, including facts about writing systems and warfare.

41. **The Bronze Age was a time in Europe when people made tools and weapons out of bronze, an alloy of copper and tin.**

42. **Bronze tools were much stronger than the stone tools that had been used before.**

43. **The oldest known writing systems in Europe emerged in the Aegean. The Linear A, Cypro-Minoan, and Cretan hieroglyph writing systems developed in Europe** during the first half of the second millennium BCE.

44. **The oldest known writing system in Europe that has been fully deciphered is called Linear B,** which dates back to about 1400 BCE during the Late Bronze Age in Greece.

45. **The Linear B script was deciphered in 1952 and consists of more than eighty syllable signs,** as well as more than one hundred ideograms that denote objects in writing and cannot be pronounced phonetically.

46. **Bronze smelting gradually spread throughout Western Eurasia.** Some evidence indicates that it might have been independently developed multiple times at different places within the region.

47. **From about 3500 BCE, it spread gradually throughout Europe,** from southeastern parts such as the Aegean Islands, the Balkans, and the Caucasus to western Europe.

48. **The Bronze Age was a period of great social change in Europe.** New forms of government emerged, and large cities were built, such as Knossos on the island of Crete.

49. **Archaeologists have found evidence that some communities during the Bronze Age buried their dead in tombs filled with valuable objects like jewelry or weapons made from bronze.**

50. **The Bronze Age saw an expansion in trade and commerce** due to the increased availability of metal tools and weapons.

51. **Clear evidence of warfare has been found throughout Europe** from this era, suggesting that conflict was commonplace.

52. **Bronze swords were used by European armies during the Bronze Age.**

53. **Women played an important role in society.** They could be priestesses or even rulers! However, men tended to rule the most often.

54. **Bronze was used to produce jewelry and artwork like gold ornaments and decorated shields.**

55. **It is believed the first complex European civilizations started to emerge during the Bronze Age,** likely due to the technological and cultural advancements that made it possible to live sustainably in large communities.

56. **Initially, these civilizations were located around the Mediterranean Sea** because of the more favorable living conditions and proximity to other civilizations in Egypt and Mesopotamia.

57. **By the end of this era, the chariot was becoming an important part of warfare and transportation** due to its speed on rough terrain when compared with walking or riding horseback.

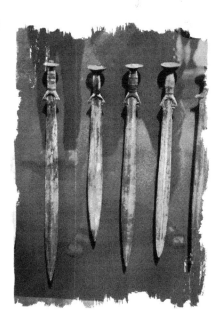

58. **Pottery production experienced rapid growth,** with vessels becoming much larger and more complexly decorated.

59. **The use of bronze tools allowed humans to do things like mine and build complex structures and weapons** that were much more efficient than previous versions.

60. **The Bronze Age ended when iron replaced bronze as the metal of choice** for tools and weapons, ushering in a new age known as the Iron Age.

The Rise of the Minoan Civilization
(c. 3000–1100 BCE)

This chapter will explore the incredible history of the Minoan civilization, one of the first major civilizations in Europe. We'll take a look at an impressive array of facts about their culture, beliefs, and arts. Uncover why this ancient society had such a huge impact on later civilizations like ancient Greece and Rome.

61. **The Minoan civilization is often considered the first civilization in Europe.** It began around 3000 BCE.

62. **The Minoans were mainly farmers who lived on islands off the coast of mainland Greece, such as Crete.**

63. **They built impressive palaces with large courtyards, storerooms, workshops, and private apartments for royalty or important people.** Minoan palaces have been found at **Knossos and Phaistos.**

64. **The Minos Palace on the island of Knossos,** for example, is a site that served both as a religious and an administrative center, and was not only used for royal residence – being a testament to **the sophisticated Minoan culture.**

65. **They developed the Linear A script,** which has still not been fully deciphered by modern scholars.

66. **Their culture is believed to have been based on maritime trade due to their location near the Mediterranean Sea.** They were connected to other civilizations, such as Egypt, Syria, and Anatolia.

67. **The Minoans had a rich art tradition that included pottery making, metalworking, and jewelry-making.** Many of these surviving artifacts are now housed in museums around the world.

68. **They were known for their beautiful frescoes and intricate relief designs** that depicted scenes of nature, people, and animals.

69. The Minoans are believed to have invented true fresco, a technique that results in the pigment becoming part of the wall.

70. They believed in many gods, including ones that represented nature. For instance, they believed snakes represented fertility and bulls for strength.

71. They developed advanced architectural techniques, such as archways and columns to support the weight of buildings, some of which reached up to three stories!

72. The Minoan civilization is famous for having one of the oldest labyrinths ever built. This winding maze full of secret passages and chambers is thought to have been located in Crete's Palace of Knossos.

73. Unlike other ancient civilizations, women often held higher positions than men in society. Some even served as priestesses at important religious sites like the Palace of Knossos.

74. The Minoans built complex irrigation systems to bring fresh water into cities and surrounding areas, which allowed them to develop and advance agricultural methods.

75. They were skilled seafarers. Their ships even traveled as far away as Egypt and Syria!

76. The civilization was named after Minos, a figure in Greek mythology who was a king of Crete and the son of Zeus and Europa.

77. The Minoan civilization declined after c. 1450 BCE. For the next few centuries, it would be dominated and eventually taken over politically and culturally by the Mycenaean civilization from mainland Greece.

78. It is also thought the Minoan culture was destroyed by natural disasters, such as earthquakes and volcanic eruptions, which caused massive destruction to their cities.

79. In c. 1600 BCE, for example, the eruption of the Thera volcano is believed to have caused an ecological catastrophe in the region.

80. We know much more about this civilization today thanks to Sir Arthur Evans, who discovered many artifacts during archaeological excavations between 1900 and 1930 CE.

Mycenaean Civilization
(1750–1050 BCE)

Discover the fascinating history of the Mycenaean civilization. We'll explore twenty interesting facts about their lifestyle, including how they were heavily influenced by the Minoan civilization.

81. **The Mycenaeans were an ancient civilization that lived during the Bronze Age in Greece** from around 1750 to 1050 BCE.

82. **While the Minoans lived on the Greek islands, the Mycenaeans lived mostly in mainland Greece.**

83. **Their culture was heavily influenced by the Minoan civilization.** Both civilizations shared similar styles of pottery, jewelry, and other artifacts, as well as religious rituals and customs.

84. **Because of this, the Mycenaean civilization is sometimes referred to as the successor of the Minoan civilization.**

85. **Scholars believe that Homer's epic stories, such as the Odyssey and the Iliad,** were inspired by actual events that took place during this period.

86. **Archaeologists have uncovered many tombs and sites throughout Greece belonging to Mycenaean rulers and nobles.** They have found various gold artifacts, weapons, and armor.

87. **The Mycenaeans were prolific traders with other nearby civilizations, such as Egypt, the Hittite Empire, and Anatolia.** They exchanged goods for precious metals like copper, bronze, and tin.

88. **When it comes to political organization, the Mycenae king, called the wanax, combined military, political, and religious roles. He ruled the Mycenean state.**

89. **Their economy was based largely on agriculture.** They grew wheat, barley, olives, and grapes to produce wine or olive oil that was exported around the Mediterranean region.

90. **Warfare played an essential role in their society.** Warriors would use chariots drawn by horses or oxen during battle. **The Mycenaeans** would be armed with swords, spears, or bows and arrows.

91. **Pottery from this period depicts scenes from daily life,** such as farmers working in the fields, fishermen out at sea catching their dinner, or people attending religious ceremonies.

92. **The Mycenaeans developed much of the ancient Greek mythology and worshiped gods such as Zeus, Poseidon, Artemis, and Hera.** Sacrifices were made to appease these deities.

93. **Their architecture was quite advanced for the period.** Large palaces with vaulted ceilings made from **stone blocks called megarons** could be found at nearly every major Mycenaean site in Greece!

94. **The archeological sites of Mycenae and Tiryns, located in the Peloponnese,** are the two places that contain the best evidence of this period, including ancient ruins that still stand strong today.

95. **The term "Mycenaean" is derived from the Greek city of Mycenae, one of their most powerful strongholds and home to legendary King Agamemnon,** the leader during the Trojan War.

96. **Agamemnon, as well as other figures from Mycenaean history, are believed to be half-real and half-legends.** These figures are often mentioned in mythological stories.

97. **The Mycenaeans made fine jewelry using gold, silver, and other precious stones like lapis lazuli or carnelian.**

98. **Their art and designs were characterized by geometric shapes, such as circles, triangles, spirals, and zigzags.**

99. **Mycenaean language was part of the larger Proto-Indo-European language family,** containing

characteristics that were lost over time and did not emerge in the later Ancient Greek.

100. **The Mycenaean civilization eventually began to decline sometime around 1200 BCE during the Bronze Age Collapse.** This event is still mysterious, but many speculate that it was caused by natural disasters or even invasions from foreign tribes.

Ancient Greece
(800–146 BCE)

This chapter will dive into the captivating history of ancient Greece. We'll explore twenty interesting facts about their culture, beliefs, and government. The Greeks laid some very important foundations; it's time to take a look at how influential they were!

101. After the Bronze Age Collapse, the people who inhabited modern-day Greece, **the Aegean Islands, and parts of eastern Anatolia entered a period of decline called the Greek Dark Ages.**

102. **The people in these lands referred to themselves as Hellenes and the land they lived in as Hellas.** They spoke the same language and shared much of their culture, contributing to the formation of a common identity.

103. **However, ancient Greece was not a unified state or an empire.** Instead, ancient Greece consisted of many city-states, each with its own form of government.

104. **Two of the most city-states were Athens and Sparta. Athens had an early form of democracy, and Sparta was ruled by two kings.**

105. **The Greek city-states began to emerge after the end of the Greek Dark Ages,** beginning around 800 BCE.

106. **Over the next few centuries, the city-states rapidly developed the Greek culture and society.** Ancient Greece arguably became the most advanced civilization of its time.

107. **The Greeks believed in living a balanced life, with physical activity, education, religion, and art** all playing important roles in everyday life.

108. **They practiced science and mathematics,** leading to advances in astronomy, engineering, medicine, and more.

109. **Ancient Greek culture was spread through trade with other regions,** creating a cultural exchange that can still be seen in modern-day Europe and beyond.

110. **Some Greek city-states like Athens had a well-developed system of law courts** that allowed citizens to access justice without fear of punishment from rulers.

111. **Ancient Greece had an alphabet that was adapted from Phoenician traders.** It featured influences from earlier scripts of the region and, in its modified form, is still used for writing in Greek to this day.

112. **The Greeks worshiped gods like Zeus, Athena, Apollo, and Aphrodite.** These deities were made into statues and other artworks. The Greeks also had temples, like the Parthenon in Athens, which still stands today.

113. **The ancient Greeks built stadiums for sporting events** where thousands would come to watch competitions between athletes worldwide.

114. **In Olympia in 776 BCE, the first Olympic Games took place.** They would be held every four years for twelve centuries!

115. **Advances in political and social thought, as well as in philosophy,** helped create a complex Greek society that influenced neighboring civilizations.

116. **Ancient Greece is well known for its thinkers, such as Socrates, Plato, and Aristotle.** These men contributed greatly to the study of the world.

117. **Greek philosophers wrote about human nature, ethics, and government in books like the Republic.** These writings are still used today to understand politics.

118. **The Greeks created masterpieces of art, including sculptures depicting gods and heroes from mythology, pottery painted with beautiful scenes,** and intricate jewelry crafted out of gold or silver.

119. **Architects built theaters where plays were performed for large audiences.** Some famous ancient Greek playwrights include Sophocles and Euripides.

120. **Ancient Greece was the birthplace of Western civilization. Its ideas, art, language, and literature shaped much of Europe and even parts of Asia.**

The Greco-Persian Wars
(499–449 BCE)

The Greco-Persian Wars was a major conflict between the ancient Greek city-states and the Persian Empire. This section will explore twenty facts about this important conflict, such as why war broke out.

121. **The Greco-Persian Wars were a series of wars fought between the Greek city-states and the Persian Empire.** The wars started in 499 BCE and ended in 449 BCE.

122. **This conflict is also known as the Persian Wars or the Great War.** The battles in these wars took place both on land and at sea.

123. **At its peak, Persia stretched from the Balkan states in Europe to India and south to Egypt.** It was a powerful player in the Middle East.

124. **Two of the most powerful city-states at this time in ancient Greece were Athens and Sparta, exerting their influence on neighboring smaller city-states.** They led the Greek resistance against the Persians.

125. **The region of the Peloponnese was dominated by Sparta, a military powerhouse,** which founded the Peloponnesian League in the 6th century BCE – an alliance mainly consisting of the region's independent city-states.

126. **The initial cause of the war stemmed from disagreements over trading rights within Ionia** (modern-day Turkey).

127. **Persian rulers Darius I and Xerxes would try on different occasions to launch invasions into mainland Greece** and get the city-states to submit to Persian rule. However, these invasions would eventually end in failure.

128. **The Greeks won despite being outnumbered because they used clever tactics,** such as delaying the Persians long enough to gain help from their allies.

129. **One of the most famous battles in these wars was the Battle of Marathon, which took place in 490 BCE.** The Greek army defeated the invading Persian force by using superior strategy and tactics.

130. **The modern marathon was inspired by the Battle of Marathon. Pheidippides, Athens's greatest runner, is said to have run from Marathon to Athens to deliver news of the victory of the Battle of Marathon.** When he announced the victory, he fell down, dead.

131. **The Greeks' victories at sea were mainly due to their smaller but more agile ships** that could outmaneuver larger Persian vessels.

132. **Sparta was one of the main Greek forces that fought against Persia during this period.** Sparta was well known for its military tradition and well-trained hoplites.

133. **During the Greco-Persian Wars, a famous Athenian leader named Themistocles** used a naval strategy to defeat a much larger Persian fleet at Salamis in 480 BCE.

134. **The Battle of Thermopylae in 480 BCE is another battle from these wars that has become legendary.** The movie 300 was loosely based on the conflict. Three hundred Spartan warriors, seven hundred Thespians, and hundreds of helots stood against an overwhelming number of Persians. The Greeks were fought to the death.

135. **In 479 BCE, Greece experienced its greatest victory over the Persians at the Battle of Plataea** when 10,000 Greeks defeated 100,000 Persians led by Xerxes.

136. **In 478, Athens founded the Delian League, a confederation of Greek city-states with the purpose of fighting the Persian Empire.** The Delian League included many Greek islands in the Aegean, resulting in it emerging as the most powerful naval force in the region.

137. **The war ended when both sides agreed to end hostilities through the Peace of Callias in c. 449 BCE.** The peace granted autonomy to Ionian city-states and settlements in Asia Minor, with Persian ships being excluded from entering the Aegean.

138. **Following the conclusion of these wars,** Athens became one of the main powers in the ancient Mediterranean world.

139. **In the aftermath of the Greco-Persian Wars,** Greece experienced its golden age. This period saw art, literature, and philosophy flourish.

140. **The aftermath of the Greco-Persian Wars also saw the escalation between the two alliances led by Athens and Sparta,** concluding in the outbreak of the Peloponnesian War between the two sides in 431.

141. **This conflict lasted until 404 BCE and proceeded in a series of phases,** during which the two sides vied for hegemony and influence in the ancient Greek world.

142. **Spartans adopted an aggressive policy and attacked the Athenians and their allies** with the heavy hoplite units that were considered to have been among the best soldiers of the ancient world.

143. **Athenian strategy, on the other hand,** was containment on land and reliance on naval attacks and blockades, as **the Athenian-led Delian League** was superior in the sea.

144. **The Peloponnesian War ended in the defeat of Athens and its allies** in 404 BCE, with Sparta emerging as the new hegemon in ancient Greece for a time.

145. **About a hundred years after the conclusion of the Greco-Persian Wars, Alexander the Great from the Kingdom of Macedon** would unite almost all of Greece and end the Persian Empire.

Alexander the Great and the Hellenic League

This concise overview navigates through pivotal events, from post-Peloponnesian War turbulence to Philip II of Macedon's ambitions. Explore the extraordinary reign of **Alexander the Great**, whose conquests reshaped the ancient world, leaving behind a legacy of Hellenization.

146. After the end of **the Peloponnesian War**, Athens was briefly ruled by a group of oligarchs known as **the Thirty Tyrants.**

147. **The Thirty Tyrants were installed by Sparta** to keep the city-state under Spartan influence.

148. **The Thirty Tyrants were overthrown a year later.** Spartan dominance in the region was challenged by **the Corinthian War** (395–387 BCE).

149. During this war, **Athens, aided by the city-states of Corinth, Argos, and Thebes, fought Sparta.** They were unable to achieve a decisive victory, ultimately leading to the weakening of both sides.

150. **The Peace of Antalcidas was concluded in 387 BCE** after the Persian Empire intervened on the side of the allied city-states and aided them against the Spartans.

151. **After the conclusion of the war, the city-state of Thebes** was able to exploit the weakened state of Sparta and rebelled against Spartan hegemony in 378 BCE.

152. **Thebes was able to defeat Sparta in the Battle of Leuctra** in 371 BCE, leading to a brief period of Theban hegemony over Greece, which lasted until 362 BCE.

153. In 362, **the Battle of Mantinea** took place. Epaminondas, a leader who helped Thebes rise to power, died in the battle. This led to a decline in Theban power.

154. **Instability in the region resulted in significantly weaker Greek city-states** by the mid-4th century BCE compared to their state prior to the beginning of the Greco-Persian Wars.

155. **The instability also led to the rise of Panhellenic ideas among the Greeks,** preferring political unity instead of the current status quo of city-states.

156. **The Kingdom of Macedon, a Hellenistic kingdom located in the north centered around the city of Pella,** began to rise to power in the mid- to late 4th century BCE.

157. **Macedon had remained neutral for most of the wars in Greece** and was in a more powerful position to emerge as a dominant force in Greece by the end of the century.

158. **King Philip II of Macedon decided to impose his influence over the other city-states,** partly to unite them against the looming Persian threat.

159. **King Philip formed the League of Corinth, an alliance of city-states under Macedon.** It held its first council in Corinth after Philip's forces emerged victorious in the Battle of Chaeronea in 338 BCE against Thebes and Athens.

160. **The Macedonian king proposed a defensive alliance among the southern Greek city-states** (except for Sparta, which refused). He refused to impose his authority through military means.

161. **He was succeeded by his son and designated heir Alexander III,** who would come to be known as **Alexander the Great.** He would become one of the most accomplished rulers of all time.

162. **Alexander's first policy was to subdue the Greek city-states,** and he campaigned extensively during the first few years of his reign in the Balkans.

163. In 335 BCE, **Alexander decisively defeated the Thebans and destroyed the city of Thebes,** something that forced other city-states to submit to Alexander.

164. **Alexander was also able to secure the frontier provinces with Persian possessions** in Asia Minor for his war against the Achaemenids.

165. **Alexander was able to achieve a complete conquest of the vast Persian Empire** by the time of his unexpected death in 323 BCE.

166. **Alexander achieved decisive victories in the battles of Granicus** (334 BCE), **Issus** (333 BCE), **Tyre and Gaza** (332 BCE), and **Gaugamela** (331 BCE), which allowed him to overwhelm Persian resistance and claim Persian lands for himself.

167. **Entering victorious in Persian satrapies in Asia Minor, the Levant, Egypt, and Iran, Alexander was accepted as the new leader** and emerged as one of the most powerful figures of all of antiquity.

168. **Alexander's conquests reached as far as the Indus River in the east.**

169. **Alexander died in Babylon in 323 BCE.** It is not known for sure what caused his death, but most scholars believe he died of typhoid fever or some other illness.

170. **Alexander's empire disintegrated soon after his death.** The territories he had gained were split among his generals in **the Wars of the Diadochi.**

171. **His conquests caused massive sociocultural shifts throughout the ancient world.** It resulted in the influx of Greek settlers in these lands and a subsequent process of Hellenization, the spread of Greek culture and traditions.

172. **Ancient Greek became the lingua franca of the ancient world.** Greek customs were fused with rich local traditions to produce unique regional variations for the next few hundred years.

173. **The resulting Hellenistic period was marked by great achievements in arts, science, and philosophy.**

174. **The polities that succeeded Alexander's empire** eventually became too unstable and were conquered by the Romans.

175. **The ancient Greek world left behind an astonishing legacy** that stands as a testament to the importance of this era in European and world history.

The Roman Republic
(509–27 BCE)

This chapter will explore the incredible history of the Roman Republic, another early great civilization in Europe. We'll take a look at twenty-five interesting facts about their government, religions, engineering feats, and more!

176. **The city of Rome was legendarily founded in 753 BCE by twin brothers named Remus and Romulus.**

177. **The Roman civilization quickly grew from the city of Rome**, occupying most of central Italy by the 6th century BCE.

178. **The Romans battled other people groups living in the peninsula,** including the Etruscans, who were mostly concentrated in the north, and Greek city-states in the south.

179. **The Romans spoke the Latin language, which was originally a dialect spoken in the Latium region in central Italy.**

180. **Through military victories over their neighbors,** the Romans would emerge as the most dominant power in Italy. **The Latin culture** was later spread around other parts of the world by the Romans.

181. **Unlike ancient Greece, Rome was initially a kingdom. Its last king, Tarquinius Superbus,** was overthrown around 509 BCE, and a republic was established.

182. **The word "republic" comes from the Latin res publica, meaning "public affair."** It is a state where political power is supposed to be held by the people.

183. **The Romans were greatly influenced by the Greek culture and way of life.** They adopted a political system similar to that of the Greeks, as well as their complex system of gods.

184. The Roman gods governed over different aspects of life, like war, agriculture, or death, much like the Greek gods. The Roman gods corresponded to the Greek gods, except most had different names. For example, Zeus was called Jupiter.

185. The Romans established a legislative branch called the Senate, which was composed of tens and then hundreds of citizens who were chosen by the consuls and served for life as magistrates.

186. The consuls were the two leaders of the Roman Republic. They served one-year terms. They had a special power called veto, which meant they could stop their colleague from doing something if it was a bad idea.

187. The Roman Republic was divided into two classes: the patricians, who were wealthy landowners and business owners, and the plebeians, who were commoners or peasants who worked on farms or in businesses owned by the patricians.

188. The Roman Republic was divided into different provinces, which were ruled by governors who had been appointed by the Senate in Rome.

189. The earliest written legislation of Rome was the Twelve Tables, which was first promulgated in c. 450 BCE. They reconfirmed the class distinctions between the plebeians and the patricians and recognized the rights of each.

190. The Romans were great engineers. They built roads, some of which still stand today. They also built aqueducts to move water from place to place, bridges across rivers, and walls around their cities for protection against enemies.

191. All citizens of the Roman Republic had certain rights, including the right to vote on laws and elect officials who would lead them.

192. Not everyone could be a citizen. You had to be male, and both your parents had to be Roman. Later on, the senators and even emperors would grant citizenship to people living in the Roman Empire.

193. **Gladiator fights were popular entertainment among Romans.** These fighters fought each other using weapons like swords or spears at events held in large arenas.

194. **The Romans built one of the first versions of a sewer system to remove waste from public areas in their cities.**

195. **Romans paid a lot of attention to learning and science,** much like the Greeks, leaving behind a rich cultural legacy.

196. **Rome was notorious for its professional military,** which was one of the key reasons behind its formation as a powerful state.

197. **The Roman legions created complex formations called tortoises,** which allowed the soldiers to move around on battlefields while being protected and having access to their weapons during battle if needed.

198. **The ancient Romans had many different types of soldiers, including cavalry** (horse-mounted warriors), **infantry** (soldiers who fought on foot), **and auxiliaries** (non-Roman citizens who served as soldiers).

199. **While the Romans did not invent concrete,** they were the first to use it for most of their construction projects, which included amphitheaters, temples, and aqueducts.

200. **After the establishment of the republic, Rome expanded its territories,** emerging as masters of Italy, southern Iberia, and the North African coast. It would later become one of the greatest empires in world history.

The Roman Empire
(27 BCE–476 CE)

The Roman Empire is one of the most iconic and influential periods in all of history. Spanning from 27 BCE to 476 CE, this period saw vast expansion and a flourishing culture. Let's explore twenty facts about the Roman Empire!

201. **By the 1st century BCE, Rome had expanded rapidly, taking over Greece and parts of Anatolia.** It also controlled Iberia and North Africa.

202. **The Senate had to govern a very large territory,** which was practically impossible. Local commanders and generals held a lot of power in the Roman provinces.

203. During the 1st century BCE, **the Roman Republic suffered from internal conspiracies and civil wars.** The generals continued expanding their power.

204. **Julius Caesar, one of the most powerful generals who conquered Gaul,** marched his forces into Rome. He took control of the republic in 45 BCE.

205. **Julius Caesar was assassinated in 44 BCE by the senators.** Different factions formed, but Julius Caesar's adopted son and successor, Augustus (formerly known as Octavian), declared himself emperor in 27 BCE by order of the Senate.

206. **Augustus was granted the title of princeps** (first citizen) and became the de facto ruler of all of Rome.

207. **The Julio-Claudian dynasty, founded by Augustus,** included emperors such as **Tiberius, Caligula, Claudius, and Nero.**

208. **The Senate still existed, but it did not have that much power.** Augustus reduced the number of senators from nine hundred to six hundred.

209. At its height, **the Roman Empire stretched from Britain to North Africa and parts of Asia Minor** (modern-day Turkey).

210. **During the Pax Romana** (the Roman Peace), which lasted from 27 BCE to 180 CE, there was stability in the Roman Empire, although wars with outside forces still occurred.

211. **From the late 1st to the 2nd century CE, Rome was ruled by five consecutive emperors,** who are sometimes referred to as the Five Good Emperors.

212. **This term was coined by Niccolo Machiavelli in the 16th century** to describe the period of stability under the emperors Nerva, Trajan, Hadrian, Antoninus Pius, and Marcus Aurelius.

213. **Machiavelli claimed that the Roman Empire prospered because the emperors chose their heirs;** the throne wasn't inherited at that time.

214. **Trajan, emperor from 98 to 117 CE, expanded the Roman Empire to its greatest territorial extent,** including the conquest of Dacia (modern-day Romania) and parts of Mesopotamia.

215. **Marcus Aurelius, who reigned from 161 to 180 CE, was not only one of the most successful emperors of Rome** but also made a name for himself due to his contributions to the philosophy of Stoicism.

216. **His Meditations, a series of personal writings in Koine Greek that were composed by the emperor for his own personal use,** has become one of the best-selling philosophical books.

217. **Latin became the common language that united all people living under the rule of Rome,** which helped them stay connected.

218. **The Crisis of the Third Century (235–284 CE) was a period of political, military,** and economic instability characterized by frequent changes of emperors and invasions by external tribes.

219. **In order to better control the vast territories of the Empire, Emperor Diocletian** introduced a system called the Tetrarchy in 286 CE.

220. **The Tetrarchy was a division of Roman lands into two administrative units of East and West,** each ruled by a separate augustus. Some later emperors became rulers of both parts.

221. **Diocletian also introduced several other administrative and economic reforms that helped stabilize the situation of the empire during the late third century.**

222. **The division of the empire was made final in 395 upon the death of Emperor Theodosius I,** the last emperor of united Rome. His sons, Honorius and Arcadius, emerged as the emperors of the Western and Eastern Roman Empires, respectively.

223. **Emperor Constantine the Great,** who ruled from 306 to 337 CE, constructed a new imperial residence at **the Bosphorus Strait.** This city, Constantinople, became the capital of the Eastern Roman Empire.

224. **Christianity was initially persecuted by the emperors. Nero** and others were infamous for their brutal treatment and hatred toward the Christians.

225. **Constantine the Great legalized Christianity with the Edict of Milan** in 313 CE, which ended the persecution of Christians in the empire.

226. **In 380 CE, Emperor Theodosius declared Christianity the official state religion,** something that was followed by a gradual rooting out of Roman pagan practices throughout the empire's territories.

227. **Hadrian's Wall was built by the Romans in 122 CE** to protect against the barbarians in northern England and Scotland.

228. In 475 CE, **Romulus Augustus became the last emperor of the Western Roman Empire.** His reign ended a year later when Rome was invaded by the barbarian general Odoacer.

229. After 476 CE, **power shifted away from Rome.** Smaller kingdoms were formed that controlled different sections of Europe.

230. **The fall of the Roman Empire led to the Middle Ages,** a period in Europe when there was less centralized government and more reliance on local rulers for protection.

The Migration Period
(375–700 CE)

This chapter will explore the Migration Period in Europe, a period of intense movement and change. We'll take a look at twenty interesting facts about how these migrations influenced Europe.

231. **The Migration Period refers to a time of large-scale westward migrations of different eastern European tribal peoples.**

232. **The Migration Period resulted in barbarian invasions in the lands of the Roman Empire.** Some of these tribes, such as the Ostrogoths and Visigoths, were involved in the fall of the Western Roman Empire in 476.

233. **It is hard to know for sure how many people migrated during this time,** but estimates don't go above 750,000.

234. **Germanic tribes migrated into northern and western Europe from their homeland near the Black Sea region in eastern Europe.**

235. **These tribes included the Visigoths, Franks, Vandals, and Angles.** They invaded Roman territories in Italy, Gaul, Iberia, and even North Africa.

236. **Romans referred to all non-Roman peoples as barbarians,** and they implemented different policies in dealing with them.

237. **Although the Roman Empire conquered many barbarian territories,** it sometimes allowed neighboring barbarians to come and settle in lands controlled by Rome.

238. **Rome was sacked four times by the barbarians. The Visigoth attack on Rome** in 410 is often viewed as the beginning of the end of the Roman Empire.

239. **The Roman forces had a hard time controlling the barbarians.** Rome was also dealing with internal instability, civil wars, and an economic crisis.

240. **One of the major reasons the barbarians started moving westward was because of the Huns.** They made devastating attacks on people living in eastern Europe, forcing them to move out of the region.

241. **In 476, after about two centuries of dealing with large-scale barbarian invasions, Germanic King Odoacer deposed the last Western Roman emperor.** The rest of the empire disintegrated very quickly.

242. **The migrating tribes settled in different former Roman provinces and started to establish state-like formations** that were separate from each other.

243. **The Eastern Roman Empire was relatively unaffected by barbarian invasions and managed to survive the Migration Period intact.**

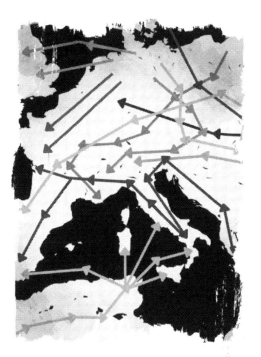

244. **The Migration Period led to the collapse of the Roman Latin culture** and the rise in the prominence of Germanic cultures.

245. **The new rulers tried to adopt former Roman customs and traditions to legitimize themselves as new leaders,** though this was only partially successful.

246. **Christianity strengthened these local authorities.** They used religious doctrine to control populations.

247. **The barbarian invasions led to a fragmentation of political authority, as individual leaders grew more powerful than before.** Local rulers became increasingly influential within their regions.

248. By 568, **most of the Germanic tribes had settled down in their new homelands.** The period of migration slowed down significantly.

249. **It is believed the Migration Period helped give rise to modern nation-states** by creating distinct ethnic and linguistic boundaries in Europe.

250. **The Migration Period saw a decline in trade and commerce as people moved away from cities,** resulting in economic instability throughout Europe.

The Early Middle Ages
(476–1000 CE)

The Early Middle Ages, sometimes called the Dark Ages, was a time of great transformation. This chapter will explore twenty fascinating facts about this era in history, from the spread of Christianity to technological advances. Let's see what this era was all about!

251. **The Early Middle Ages, which is part of the medieval period,** lasted from 476 to 1000 CE in Europe.

252. **This period is also known as the "Dark Ages"** because learning and culture declined due to invasions from groups like the Vikings, Muslims, and Magyars (Hungarians).

253. Many historians today dislike using **the term "Dark Ages" because it implies Europe was culturally stagnant during this time,** which was not the case

254. **The fall of the Western Roman Empire is traditionally seen as the beginning of the Early Middle Ages.**

255. **Overall, the Early Middle Ages was a time of instability and uncertainty in Europe as new states were formed on the remnants of the old Roman Empire.**

256. **Feudalism became a popular political and economic system during this time. People gave their loyalty to lords** in exchange for protection and land rights.

257. **Christianity spread throughout Europe, eventually replacing other religions, like the Norse religion.** It took centuries for Christianity to be accepted by most of a people group.

258. **The Anglo-Saxons converted relatively quickly to Christianity.** Most Anglo-Saxons were practicing Christians roughly a century after it had been introduced to England!

259. **The Roman Church saw itself as the symbolic successor to the Roman Empire.** It gained power and wealth during the medieval period.

260. **The church sent missionaries to different parts of Europe to spread Christianity and convert the pagan rulers.** One of the most missionaries was Saint Augustine, who brought Christianity to England in 597.

261. **The people built churches and cathedrals, which became important social centers for their communities.** People could gather there to worship or trade goods with each other at markets nearby.

262. **Monasteries became popular centers for learning in medieval Europe. Monks helped spread Christianity.** They were known for being pious and austere individuals.

263. **The Franks adopted the Latin language after they conquered Gaul** (modern-day France) around 500 CE. They made it the official language of administration and culture in the western European states.

264. **During the Early Middle Ages, people used Roman numerals** to keep track of numbers instead of the modern-day Arabic numerals that we use today.

265. **The Franks unified parts of Europe during the Carolingian Empire** (800–843), which was later dissolved due to internal disputes and fragmentation of political power.

266. In the 5th century, **the Angles, Saxons, and Jutes invaded Britain.** These people jointly became known as **the Anglo-Saxons.** They established their own language, Old English, which later developed into modern English!

267. **The Anglo-Saxon migration into Britain forced the local Brittonic peoples to move to the peripheries of the British Isles;** their societies survived in parts of Wales, Ireland, and Scotland.

268. Around 800 CE, **knights emerged due to feudalism.** They were part-time soldiers responsible for protecting their lord's castle or estate from invaders.

269. **The Early Middle Ages saw significant technological developments,** including improved horse harnesses and stirrups, heavy plows, and horseshoes, as well as more efficient crop rotation techniques.

270. **The Reconquista was launched by the Christians in 722** in hopes of reclaiming Iberia from the Muslim conquerors.

The Byzantine Empire
(330–1453 CE)

Explore the impressive history of the Byzantine Empire with these twenty-five interesting facts! From its founding to its fall, discover how this rich culture blended religions, languages, and art throughout Europe, Africa, and Asia.

271. **The Eastern Roman Empire, also known as the Byzantine Empire, was founded in the 4th century by Emperor Constantine I.** It lasted until 1453—about one thousand years after the fall of the Western Roman Empire!

272. **The name comes from the old Greek city of Byzantium,** which served as the site for the empire's capital, Constantinople.

273. **Constantinople was the center of Europe during the Middle Ages.** It was the largest and the richest city, with walls that were about forty feet high.

274. **At the time of its split from the Western Roman Empire,** the Byzantine Empire controlled lands in the Balkans, Anatolia, the Near East, and Egypt. It was far richer and more powerful than its western counterpart.

275. **The Byzantine Empire considered itself the rightful successor of Rome after its fall.** Many attempts were made to assert Byzantine authority in Europe during the Middle Ages.

276. **Justinian I, who reigned from 527 to 565, was able to take control of parts of Italy,** North Africa, and Iberia.

277. **Justinian is remembered as the ruler who tried to restore the borders of the old Roman Empire.** He is also remembered for his code of laws, which influenced many European states later on.

278. **Empress Theodora, Justinian's wife, was very influential.** She recognized the rights of women and used her influence to pass religious and social reforms.

279. **Despite Justinian's efforts, the Byzantine Empire was unable to assert its dominance over the rest of Europe.** The cultural differences between the Byzantine Empire and post-Roman western Europe would grow.

280. **The Byzantine Empire is known for its unique blend of cultures and religions,** but it was primarily a Greek state.

281. **Byzantine citizens spoke a form of Greek called Byzantine Greek,** though they also knew Latin.

282. **The majority of the territories the Byzantine Empire controlled had been Hellenized during the heyday of ancient Greece and with the conquests of Alexander the Great.**

283. **A series of controversial events would lead to the "official" split of the Christian Church in 1054.** The Great Schism saw the formation of the Western Roman Catholic Church and the Eastern Orthodox Church.

284. **The two churches would emerge as rivals,** and both would try to convert pagans to their own version of Christianity.

285. **Russia adopted Christianity from the Byzantine Empire in 988 CE,** which is why the Russian Orthodox Church follows similar religious traditions today.

286. **Islam's rise in the 7th century weakened the Byzantine Empire politically.** The invading Arab armies conquered many Byzantine lands in the Near East and Egypt.

287. **Still, up until about the 11th century, the Byzantine Empire continued to be very powerful.** It was known for its great military and wealthy economy.

288. **The Byzantine Empire was known for its impressive architecture,** including famous basilicas like **the Hagia Sophia in Constantinople.**

289. **The Byzantines had a powerful navy that was able to protect their coasts and control the Mediterranean Sea.**

290. **The Byzantines were known for using Greek fire (the precursor to napalm) during battle,** which could be projected at enemy ships or onto land.

291. **The empire started to enter a period of decline with the arrival of the Turkic peoples from central Asia,** who conducted military campaigns in Byzantine lands.

292. **The Seljuk Turks took over much of Anatolia by the 13th century.**

293. **In 1254, Constantinople was sacked by the Crusading Christian forces, weakening the empire even more.**

294. **The Ottoman Turks emerged as the new rival to Constantinople** in the 14th century. **They defeated the Byzantine armies** time and time again.

295. **Constantinople's walls helped protect it from invaders multiple times. However, the city fell in 1453 when Ottoman forces** conquered the city after a fifty-three-day siege.

Viking Invasions
(790– 1066 CE)

Explore the remarkable history of the Vikings and their impact on Europe in this section! We will look at twenty fascinating facts about how they lived, their famous leaders, and some of their major gods.

296. **The Vikings came from Scandinavia.** They were prominent from the 8th to the 11th century.

297. **The Vikings were seafaring warrior Scandinavians.** Most of them farmed for a living but raided in the off-season.

298. **Their longboats were made out of wood. Their ships were called drakkars.** They were designed to travel shallow rivers and over open ocean. The Vikings could carry them overland if they had to.

299. **Viking warriors often went on voyages called raids.** They invaded many different parts of Europe in search of treasure, land, and power.

300. **The word "Viking" is derived from an Old Norse phrase meaning "pirate raid."**

301. **In 790 CE, they raided a monastery off the coast of England.** This is traditionally seen as the start of the Viking Age.

302. **Some coastal towns built walls around them for defense against raids,** but few were able to withstand the full force of the vicious Viking attacks.

303. **Although Vikings are often depicted wearing helmets with horns, there is no evidence to support that they wore helmets like this.** The helmets they wore were very simple.

304. **The Vikings were well known for their brave and bold attitude in battle. Legend says that the Vikings had berserkers,** men who would go into a trance-like state and fight until the death.

305. **One of the most famous Viking leaders was Ragnar Lodbrok** (also spelled Lothbrok). He raided Paris in 845. **He was eventually killed by King Aella** (also spelled as Aelle) of Northumbria in England.

306. **The Vikings were known for their intricate woodworking and metalwork.** They were also known for creating weapons like swords.

307. **They established trading routes all over Europe.** They first focused on regions in the Baltic Sea but later expanded to the Mediterranean.

308. **While most people think that only men could be Vikings, women could too.** There were not as many female Vikings, but there is evidence they might have taken part in raids.

309. **Most women played important roles at home, like running farms or businesses while their husbands were away at sea.** Some took advisor roles and helped plan raids.

310. **The Norse pantheon included Odin** (the god of war and wisdom), **Thor** (the god of thunder), **Loki** (the god of mischief), and **Freya** (the goddess of love).

311. **The Vikings had their own language called Old Norse.** Although it is no longer spoken today, elements of it can be found in the North Germanic languages.

312. **They believed in a place called Valhalla,** where brave warriors went after they died in battle. There, they would feast with Odin in the afterlife.

313. **Vikings were very superstitious people.** They believed that trolls, elves, dragons, and sea monsters existed.

314. **During this period, the Vikings left behind many stories in their poetry, songs, and art,** which have been passed down for hundreds of years.

315. **To this day, we celebrate Viking culture with festivals, movies, and books about them.** Two of the best examples of this are the TV show Vikings and the comic books and movies about Thor.

The Reconquista
(722–1492)

The Reconquista saw multiple Christian military campaigns aimed at reclaiming Iberia from Islamic rule. These twenty-five facts will shed some light on this turbulent period in European history.

316. **The Reconquista is the name given to a series of Christian military campaigns against the Islamic realms** in Iberia during the Middle Ages between 718 and 1492.

317. **Iberia had been conquered during the initial stage of Islamic expansion by the emerging Umayyad Caliphate** at the beginning of the 8th century.

318. **They destroyed the Visigothic Kingdom, which had ruled Iberia since the late 5th century,** and established an Islamic caliphate.

319. **The Christian Europeans saw this as a threat.** They began a series of military operations to reclaim the lands they believed had been unjustly lost to the Muslims.

320. **Visigothic elites fled to the north of the Iberian Peninsula, establishing the Kingdom of Asturias.** They saw themselves as the rightful claimants of the lands held by the Muslims.

321. **In 718 or 722, the Asturian armies defeated the Muslims at the Battle of Covadonga,** an event that is considered to be the beginning of the Reconquista.

322. **Up until the early 11th century, the Caliphate of Córdoba was the major Islamic political entity in Iberia,** controlling most of modern-day Spain and Portugal.

323. **The Caliphate of Córdoba was unsuccessful in trying to subdue Christian resistance.** It disintegrated into smaller Islamic polities due to internal conflicts.

324. **In the year 910, under the leadership of King Alfonso III, the Kingdom of Asturias was reorganized into the Kingdom of León,** having gained a significant chunk of territory in central Iberia.

325. Other Christian kingdoms, such as Castile, Navarre, and Galicia, would also emerge, taking the fight to the Muslims and gradually pushing them back.

326. These Christian kingdoms were not always allies with each other. They often strategically chose their partners to gain more territory and even went to war with each other.

327. The period between the 11th and 13th centuries saw significant advances in the Reconquista, with key victories such as the capture of Toledo in 1085 by Alfonso VI of León and Castile.

328. The Christian world supported the efforts of the Iberian kingdoms during the Reconquista, with Pope Alexander III sanctioning a war effort in 1064 to attack the Muslim city of Barbastro, which ended in a Christian victory.

329. Pope Urban II, who called for the First Crusade in 1095, encouraged the Reconquista in Iberia, offering spiritual rewards to those who participated in the fight to reclaim Christian territories.

330. Another important Christian victory came at the Battle of Las Navas de Tolosa in 1212, in which the combined Castilian, Leonese, Navarrese, and Portuguese forces defeated the army of the Muslim Almohad dynasty in Andalusia.

331. From the 12th to the 13th century, Christians were aided in their efforts by the newly established Catholic military orders in Iberia, whose mission was to fight in the name of Christianity against its enemies.

332. Orders, such as the Knights Templar and the Knights of Santiago, proved to be extremely valuable, often taking control of key fortifications and contributing professional soldiers to Iberian armies.

333. **The Iberians were also aided by the Crusaders on several occasions, most importantly in 1147 during the siege of Lisbon,** which greatly strengthened the position of the Kingdom of Portugal.

334. **The fall of Granada in 1492 marked the end of Muslim rule in Iberia.**

335. **The Catholic monarchs Isabella I of Castile and Ferdinand II of Aragon completed the Reconquista.**

336. **After the completion of the Reconquista, the victorious Christian kingdoms began to spread their own customs and traditions** that were fused with local Muslim practices that had developed in Iberia since the 8th century.

337. **The Reconquista had economic consequences, as the reconquered territories brought new resources,** trade routes, and agricultural lands under Christian control.

338. **The Reconquista led to major demographic changes,** as the Muslim population of the peninsula was slowly assimilated into Christian kingdoms. Many chose to leave, while others were forcefully expelled under the new rulers.

339. **In 1492, as many as 200,000 Castilian and Aragonese Jews,** as a result of the Alhambra Decree, were expelled.

340. **Christian rulers forced their new subjects to convert to Christianity,** a process that was accelerated by the Spanish Inquisition.

Charlemagne
(r. 768–814 CE)

Charlemagne was one of the most important rulers in European history. Let's discover the impact he made with these twenty-five facts about his reign and life.

341. **Charlemagne, or Charles the Great, was the son of King Pepin the Short,** who founded **the Carolingian Empire.**

342. **Charlemagne became the king of the Franks in 768. He would become the sole ruler of the Franks** after his co-ruler, his brother, died in 771.

343. **The Carolingian line, founded by Charlemagne's father and bearing the name of the eventual emperor,** replaced the ruling Frankish Merovingian dynasty.

344. **Charlemagne continued his father's policies, forging good relations with the Roman Church,** expanding his kingdom at the expense of the German pagans, and spreading Christianity.

345. **As a wise king and a great warrior, he conquered much of western and central Europe.**

346. **He defeated the Lombards in 774. These Germanic peoples had taken over much of Italy in the 6th century.** Charlemagne granted many of their lands to the Roman Church.

347. **He also launched an invasion of Spain,** which had become Muslim after the Arabs invaded in the 7th and the beginning of the 8th century.

348. **Charlemagne's only military defeat came at the hands of the Muslims** (known as the Moors) in the Battle of Roncevaux Pass in 778.

349. **Charlemagne waged wars in what is now modern-day Germany,** where he expelled the pagan peoples and spread Christianity.

350. **He played a major role in bringing Christianity to many parts of Europe,** which united Europe after centuries of division.

351. **He would sometimes use cruel tactics to get people to convert.** For example, he told the Saxons to either be baptized in the Christian faith or die.

352. **During the infamous Massacre of Verden, for example,** Charlemagne executed thousands of Saxons who refused to convert to Christianity in October of 782.

353. **He conquered much of modern-day western Germany.** He moved his capital to the German city of Aachen, where he would eventually be buried in 814.

354. **Charlemagne reunified much of western Europe.** He would be recognized as the first emperor of Europe after the fall of the Roman Empire.

355. **Pope Leo III crowned Charlemagne in Rome on Christmas Day in 800, granting him the title of the emperor of the Romans.** This move upset the Byzantine Empire, which saw itself as the continuation of the Roman Empire.

356. **His coronation marked the beginning of what is now known as the Holy Roman Empire,** although it would be several centuries until the Holy Roman Empire had a stable successive rule.

357. **Soon after being crowned emperor, Charlemagne** made sure that each region he ruled had laws in place so they could govern themselves better according to their needs.

358. **He established schools across Europe to educate students on religion,** administration, economics, and other subjects.

359. **For centuries, no ruler would be able to control as much territory in western Europe as Charlemagne,** something that is a testament to his incredible achievements.

360. **He also created the first successful system of taxation in Europe since the fall of Rome,** something that would be used for centuries afterward.

361. **His prosperous reign marked the beginning of what is known as the Carolingian Renaissance,** a period of great cultural and intellectual revival after the fall of Rome.

362. **Carolingian art, for example, was produced in religious institutions of Charlemagne and his heirs,** and was the highest form of Christian art in all of Europe at the time.

363. **He is nicknamed the "Father of Europe"** due to his impressive accomplishments in reuniting Europe.

364. **He was succeeded by his son Louis the Pious. The Carolingian Empire** would then be split by Charlemagne's grandchildren, which led to its demise.

365. **The successive states, East and West Francia, eventually evolved into the Holy Roman Empire and France during the later Middle Ages.**

The High Middle Ages in European History
(1000–1350 CE)

We'll take a look at twenty-five interesting facts about Europe's economy, culture, technology, and more during the High Middle Ages. Let's discover what made this era so impactful!

366. **The High Middle Ages were a period of growth and progress for Europe's economy and population.** Europe's population grew from about forty million to a little over seventy million people!

367. **During this period, political and social structures in Europe started to stabilize after the instability of the Early Middle Ages,** with new kingdoms forming all over the continent.

368. **The Carolingian Empire would be split with the Treaty of Verdun in the 9th century,** leading to the eventual establishment of the Kingdom of France and the Holy Roman Empire.

369. **William the Conqueror was a Norman ruler who conquered England in 1066 CE.** This event is known as the Norman Conquest.

370. **The English monarchy would develop over the next few centuries, with the turning point coming in 1215 when King John I in England signed the Magna Carta,** which guaranteed certain rights to citizens, such as trial by jury.

371. **The first universities were formed during the High Middle Ages. These institutions taught Latin grammar,** rhetoric, astronomy, music theory, and medicine, among other subjects.

372. **The first university in Europe was the University of Bologna.** It was established in 1088 and is still operating today.

373. The Crusades were fought by Europeans in an attempt to reclaim control over Jerusalem and other areas that had been conquered by Muslim forces centuries earlier. The First Crusade started in 1096, and the last official Crusade took place in 1271.

374. The High Middle Ages saw the rise of powerful monarchs, such as King Philip II of France and Richard I of England. These rulers were able to extend their power over large areas.

375. Christianity continued to spread throughout Europe, reaching eastern Europe and Scandinavia by the 10th century.

376. In fact, it was during this time that Christianity became an essential part of Europe, thanks to the prior efforts of Charlemagne and the quick Christianization of central and eastern European peoples during the Late and High Middle Ages.

377. The Magyar peoples organized their own kingdom, the Kingdom of Hungary, by the year 1000. They adopted Christianity.

378. Towns began to develop rapidly, and trade increased between cities across Europe.

379. An early form of banking emerged in the Italian city-states during this period because of increased merchant activity and the accumulation of wealth. The Bank of Venice would officially be established in 1587.

380. Military technology improved greatly. Knights wore heavy suits of armor made with metal plates joined together with rivets or leather straps. These suits of armor could weigh up to sixty pounds!

381. Gothic architecture became popular across Europe during the 12th century. This style is known for its large stained glass windows and tall spires reaching up toward the sky.

382. **The High Middle Ages was one of the most politically turbulent and violent periods of European history.** Many destructive wars, such as the Hundred Years' War between England and France, were fought during this time.

383. **The invention of the mechanical clock improved navigation,** making it possible to measure time more accurately than ever before.

384. **During this period, many religious orders, such as the Franciscans and Dominicans, were founded.** They sought to spread Christianity around Europe.

385. **Greater scientific knowledge was gained through translations of works from Arab scholars into Latin,** which brought about a revolution in European medicine and science.

386. **Marco Polo is thought to have traveled to China sometime in the 13th century.** He brought back tales of exotic lands filled with spices and silks, helping fuel the growth of trade between the East and the West.

387. **Literature flourished during this era. Some famous authors include Geoffrey Chaucer,** who wrote The Canterbury Tales; Dante Alighieri, who wrote the Divine Comedy; and Thomas Aquinas, who wrote the Summa Theologica.

388. **Guilds started to be formed during the High Middle Ages.** These organizations helped protect workers' rights and regulate trade between cities.

389. **In the middle of the 14th century, Europe was ravaged by the outbreak of the bubonic plague.** It was known as the Great Plague, but we know it better as the Black Death.

390. **The Black Death is thought to have caused the deaths of about a third of Europe's population.** It greatly set back technological, cultural, and social developments.

The Renaissance
(14th–17th Centuries)

The Renaissance was a period of profound cultural, artistic, and scientific changes that swept across Europe from the 14th to the 17th century. This section will explore twenty-five interesting facts about one of the most influential periods in European history.

391. **The Renaissance was a period in European history that lasted from around the late 14th to the 17th century.** It marked an era of cultural revival in art, literature, architecture, and other aspects of life.

392. **Italy was at the heart of this movement,** with cities like Florence playing an important role in its development.

393. **The Renaissance followed a period of great instability and upheaval in Europe, known as the Crisis of the Late Middle Ages,** a series of events that caused political and socioeconomic collapse during the 13 and 14th centuries.

394. **During the Renaissance, new ideas emerged, such as humanism,** which focused on humans instead of God or fate as being responsible for their actions and destiny.

395. **Many of the ancient Roman and Greek texts that had been lost** or had only been accessible to the clergy were slowly rediscovered during the Renaissance.

396. **The rediscovery of ancient texts ushered in a period of great learning,** which manifested itself in almost all fields of life.

397. **The word "Renaissance" means "rebirth."** The term refers to the rebirth of ancient Greek and Roman ideas.

398. **Several wealthy families from Italy emerged as patrons of up-and-coming artists,** most prominently the Florentine Medici family – which financed the projects of such artists as Michelangelo.

399. **During this era, artists began using techniques like perspective drawing to create more realistic paintings** that captured nature's and humans' beauty better than ever before.

400. **Previously, art only centered on depicting religious figures and lacked character and storytelling.** During the Renaissance, it focused on the human body, harkening back to the classical Greek style.

401. **Famous artists from the Renaissance include Michelangelo, Leonardo da Vinci, and Raphael,** who created marvelous pieces of art and sculptures that still dazzle viewers to this day.

402. **The printing press was invented in Germany during the Renaissance by Johannes Gutenberg.** The printing press allowed books to be printed faster than handwritten manuscripts.

403. **The Renaissance saw the invention of new instruments, such as the violin and harpsichord,** which allowed more complex musical compositions to be created.

404. **Scientists like Galileo Galilei began using telescopes to study the stars in detail,** leading Galileo to discover four moons orbiting Jupiter.

405. **Exploration was encouraged by many countries. Christopher Columbus made his famous voyage** across the Atlantic Ocean in 1492.

406. **Education systems were updated, with universities teaching students about humanist values, arts, and sciences,** in addition to theology and mathematics.

407. **The Renaissance slowly spread from Italy to central, western, and northern Europe.** Different regions experienced the Renaissance at different times. It wasn't a singular movement throughout all of Europe.

408. **In Italy, powerful merchant families like the Medici were patrons of the arts.** They funded many projects in Florence and Rome.

409. **The Catholic Church commissioned artists to create pieces for different papal residences and palaces.** The church's most famous commission is likely Michelangelo's painting on the ceiling of the Sistine Chapel.

410. **The Renaissance was full of famous writers, such as Niccolo Machiavelli and William Shakespeare.**

411. **Architecture changed, with builders creating structures using innovative techniques and displaying classical Greek and Roman influences,** such as the use of symmetrical arches, domes, pillars, and columns.

412. **People became interested in studying nature through observation rather than relying on superstition or religion,** which eventually led people toward the modern scientific methods we use today.

413. **Leonardo da Vinci studied human anatomy by dissecting animal and human bodies.** Although he never finished his book on anatomy, his ideas helped scientists make discoveries about the human body.

414. **The Renaissance saw the invention of new weapons,** such as cannons and guns, which changed how wars were fought.

415. **New trading routes opened up between Europe, Africa, and Asia,** allowing for goods like spices to become more easily accessible in European markets.

The Reformation
(16th century)

The 16th century was a period of profound transformation across Europe, and the Reformation was at its center. In this section, we will explore twenty interesting facts about the Reformation.

416. **The Protestant Reformation was an important religious movement in Europe during the 16th century,** which resulted in the Catholic Church splintering.

417. **The Reformation started when Martin Luther, a German monk and professor of theology,** posted his Ninety-five Theses on October 31st, 1517. He sought to challenge the Catholic Church's corrupt practices.

418. **There had been other, relatively minor, reform movements in Europe prior to Luther led by figures like John Wycliffe in England and the Czech Jan Hus.**

419. **Luther initially wrote the Ninety-seven Theses, which had a more theological viewpoint.** This work is largely ignored since the Ninety-five Theses is the one that started a revolution.

420. **The Protestant Reformation spread across Germany and other parts of Europe** over the next few decades.

421. **The Reformation was led by Luther and other influential figures, including Ulrich Zwingli in Switzerland and John Calvin in France.**

422. **One of Luther's problems with the Catholic Church was that it had become increasingly powerful and rich.** The church used its influence as leverage over the ordinary Christians of Europe, most of whom believed everything the church told them.

423. Luther was mainly concerned with the practice of indulgences. During the Middle Ages, people could go to church and pay for the salvation of their sins.

424. Luther wanted his followers to read and understand the scriptures in order to find true Christian values. He didn't want people to listen to only what was preached by the Catholic Church.

425. The reformers also recognized that many members of the Catholic clergy were becoming increasingly less versed in Christian doctrine and theology, as well as in their mastery of Latin.

426. Luther's doctrine of justification by faith alone was heavily influential. This idea asserted that an individual's true faith justified them in the eyes of God.

427. In 1521, **Martin Luther was excommunicated from the Catholic Church.**

428. Luther managed to spread his controversial ideas very quickly thanks to the newly invented printing press.

429. During this period, **new translations of the Bible were made in multiple languages so that people could read it for themselves** and interpret passages differently from what was traditionally taught by the church.

430. The Reformation brought about a period of religious wars in Europe between Catholics and Protestants, resulting in thousands of deaths.

431. Religious freedom and tolerance became more accepted as a result of the Reformation. The people wanted the freedom to choose which religion to follow.

432. In France, Spain, and Italy, the Catholic Church was still more dominant.

433. Most places in Germany, Scandinavia, the Low Countries, and England converted to different forms of Protestantism.

434. In England, King Henry VIII declared himself the head of the church, which resulted in the nation adopting Anglicanism (a form of Protestantism).

435. Other countries created their own national churches, such as Lutheranism or Presbyterianism, depending on who ruled the region.

436. The Reformation had a great impact on art. Artists began to create works that emphasized religious themes and stories, often in stark contrast to traditional Catholic artwork, which focused more on saints or biblical characters.

437. Music was greatly affected by the Reformation. Composers created hymns with lyrics taken directly from the scripture so ordinary laypeople could sing along while worshiping God at home or in church services.

438. The Catholic Church responded to Protestantism by trying to reform itself, leading to what is known today as **the Counter-Reformation or Catholic Reformation.** This movement brought about new laws, institutional changes, and educational reforms.

439. Ideas that began with **Luther's writings soon found their way into politics.** Elite circles began talking about more expression of individual freedoms, something that would eventually lead to the rise of democracy.

440. From the late 16th century onward, **many military conflicts between states were motivated by differences in religion, with Protestant and Catholic nations** taking up arms against each other.

The Thirty Years' War
(1618–1648)

The Thirty Years' War was one of the longest and most destructive wars in European history. This chapter will explore this major conflict with twenty interesting facts about how it started, who fought in it, and how it was resolved.

441. **The Thirty Years' War was a major conflict between Catholic and Protestant countries in Europe.** It was the last major European conflict that began because of religion.

442. **It started when the king of Bohemia and the Holy Roman emperor, Ferdinand II, tried to impose Catholicism on all his subjects in 1618.**

443. **The Protestant nobles of the empire started a rebellion, which would be dealt with by Ferdinand.**

444. In 1625, **Denmark declared war on the Holy Roman Empire, hoping to support the German princes in their anti-Catholic cause.** Sweden declared war on the Holy Roman Empire in 1629.

445. **Emperor Ferdinand's decision was very controversial since the 1555 Peace of Augsburg had guaranteed German princes the right to practice either Catholicism or Protestantism.**

446. **The war would drag in other kingdoms like France, Spain, and Poland.** These nations allied with the German princes to exploit instability and weaken the Holy Roman Empire or joined the Holy Roman Empire to fight for Catholicism.

447. **At the war's height, it involved almost every major state in Europe, with England being the notable exception.**

448. **The war lasted for thirty years** (1618–1648), making it one of the longest wars in European history.

449. **It caused widespread destruction across Germany,** resulting in famine, disease, and huge population losses of up to 40 percent.

450. **The Peace of Westphalia ended this war by granting freedom of religion to central Europe,** allowing more people to practice their faith openly without persecution or interference from rulers.

451. **This treaty also started to put an end to feudalism in Europe** and allowed for the development of stronger nation-states.

452. **The Peace of Westphalia established international boundaries that largely remain intact today,** such as those between France, Germany, Austria, and Switzerland.

453. **The war was fought mainly on German soil,** but it had a major impact on other European countries.

454. One of the most famous figures to rise from this conflict was King Gustavus Adolphus of Sweden, who is regarded as one of history's greatest generals.

455. The Thirty Years' War saw some early military innovations, such as the use of pike formations, improved artillery tactics, and better siege warfare techniques.

456. **It began a period known as the age of absolute monarchies.** Rulers had more power over their citizens than ever before, allowing them to raise taxes and levy armies with little oversight from other governing bodies or the citizens themselves.

457. **This war saw the introduction of more professional armies,** which were paid by taxes instead of relying on volunteers or conscription.

458. **The war helped usher in an era known as the Enlightenment,** a period when philosophers began questioning old ideas about politics and society.

459. **The Thirty Years' War resulted in tens of thousands of casualties for all sides;** it is estimated that up to a million people died of warfare and disease during this time, making it the largest-scale war in European history up to that point.

460. **The Thirty Years' War is often considered to be the first major conflict in the history of Europe** that was fought by the great European powers.

The Age of Exploration
(15th–17th Centuries)

The Age of Exploration was a period marked by remarkable discoveries, advancements in sailing technology, and trade networks between different countries. This chapter will explore twenty-five interesting facts about this era. Get ready for an exciting voyage into the past!

461. **The Age of Exploration was a period from the 15th to the 17th century** when people explored new lands and oceans in search of trade, wealth, and knowledge.

462. **The fall of Constantinople in 1453 led European countries to scramble to find new routes to the East after the Ottomans closed their access to the Silk Road.**

463. **Many European countries competed against each other to claim land and establish colonies** in newly discovered territories.

464. **Many consider Christopher Columbus's voyage to be the start of the Age of Exploration.** However, he was not the first European to discover the Americas. Leif Erikson, a Viking, discovered North America about one thousand years before Columbus set sail.

465. **Portuguese explorer Vasco da Gama became the first person to sail directly from Europe to India,** reaching the subcontinent in 1498 by traveling down the African coast to India's western coast via the Indian Ocean route that he had uncovered during his explorations.

466. **An Italian navigator named Amerigo Vespucci provided evidence that Columbus did not discover Asia but had reached mainland America.**

467. **The Americas get their name from Amerigo Vespucci!**

468. **Ferdinand Magellan led a fleet of ships on an epic voyage that circumnavigated the world in 1522.** His crew became the first to travel around the world by ship.

469. **Magellan would not survive the voyage, dying in the Philippines.**

470. **Hernán Cortés was a Spanish conquistador who conquered Mexico for Spain** in 1521 after defeating Aztec leader Montezuma II.

471. **Francisco Pizarro conquered Peru from the Incas in 1533** with just a few hundred men at his disposal.

472. **The European powers had a huge advantage compared to the natives thanks to their advanced military technology.** They had guns and cannons at their disposal and wore heavy armor. The natives fought back with bows and spears.

473. **The natives were also decimated by European diseases,** which reduced the number of people who could fight for the land.

474. **Some of the major diseases that were spread were smallpox, measles, and influenza.** It is believed up to 95 percent of natives living in the Americas died of disease or from conflicts.

475. **European powers, such as Portugal, Spain, England, and France, explored new lands for resources like gold and spices,** which could be sold at high prices, making these countries wealthier.

476. **The Portuguese established trading posts or fortresses throughout Africa, India, and China,** allowing them access to valuable resources.

477. **Spain emerged as the most dominant overseas empire during the early days of the Age of Exploration.**

478. **Spanish possessions included much of North, Central, and South America, in addition to the Philippines.**

479. **France, Great Britain, and eventually the Netherlands would emerge as dominant European colonizers,** following in the footsteps of the Portuguese and Spanish.

480. **Jesuit missionaries traveled to these new lands, spreading Christianity to the places they visited.**

481. **In North America, British migrants established small colonies centered** around their Protestant denominations.

482. **Globalization began because of these explorations since it allowed for the spread of new ideas,** products, technology, and religion.

483. **Maps were made with greater accuracy thanks to the data collected by navigators during their voyages.**

484. **African slaves were captured and then transported across the Atlantic or Indian Ocean,** where they would be sold as slaves and used as laborers or domestic workers in European colonies.

485. **The Age of Exploration brought remarkable advances in sailing technology,** such as better ship designs and navigation tools like the astrolabe.

The Scientific Revolution
(17th century)

The Scientific Revolution of the 17th century brought about immense changes in scientific understanding and discovery. These twenty interesting facts will shed light on the major discoveries that were made, as well as some of the influential scientists of this period.

486. **The Scientific Revolution refers to a period in European history that took mostly during the 16th and 17th centuries** when a new view of science and scientific thought became prominent, one that was free from philosophy and religion and was based on the scientific method.

487. **Scientists like Galileo, Johannes Kepler, and Isaac Newton** made huge advances in understanding the world around them. They used observation and experimentation instead of relying on ancient texts or superstitions.

488. **In 1610, Galileo used his telescope to observe four moons orbiting Jupiter;** he named them after figures from Greek mythology.

489. **Johannes Kepler discovered three laws of motion that helped explain why planets move in an elliptical shape around the sun** as opposed to in perfect circles, which had been believed since antiquity.

490. **Isaac Newton developed calculus, which allowed for more accurate calculations when studying movement,** such as gravity, along with forces acting upon objects.

491. **Newton developed his famous law of universal gravitation,** stating all objects attract each other through gravitational force depending on their mass.

492. **New ideas were spread across Europe due to developments in printing technology,** which allowed scientists' work to be published for wider audiences.

493. **By the end of the Scientific Revolution,** scientists had begun to use hypotheses and theories as tools to gain a deeper understanding of nature.

494. In the 1600s, **William Harvey discovered how blood circulates in human bodies by experimenting with animals like dogs and chickens.**

495. **Robert Boyle developed a law called Boyle's Law,** which states that pressure and volume are related when it comes to gases. This later became known as one of the most important laws of physics!

496. **Antonie Van Leeuwenhoek used the microscope he invented to observe bacteria,** red blood cells, spermatozoa, capillaries, and other small organisms for the first time.

497. **Antoine Lavoisier is considered the father of modern chemistry** due to his development of chemical nomenclature (names) and methods like oxidation, which changed how people studied matter.

498. **William Gilbert studied magnetism and electricity in depth.** He wrote a book on the subject called De Magnete, which helped others understand how these forces worked together.

499. **Francis Bacon developed an approach to scientific research known as empiricism,** which involves using observation and experimentation rather than relying solely on ancient texts or superstition to find answers about natural phenomena.

500. **Blaise Pascal made major contributions to mathematics and physics,** being one of the most avid defenders of the scientific method.

501. **René Descartes is most famous for developing the idea of "cogito ergo sum,"** or "I think, therefore I am," though he also made significant contributions to the field of mathematics through his development of Cartesian or analytic geometry.

502. **Ole Roemer developed a new way of measuring longitude,** which helped improve navigation on ships. He also studied light speed and made calculations about Earth's motion around the sun.

503. **Institutions such as the French Academy of Sciences in Paris and the Royal Society of London** for Improving Natural Knowledge helped accelerate scientific research and make the knowledge available to the masses.

504. **All of these new discoveries questioned the strength and legitimacy of old institutions,** most notably the church.

505. **Although women made some important contributions, they were not allowed to join the prestigious societies.** One important female thinker from this time was Maria Sibylla Merian, whose research on insects led to the discovery of life cycles.

The Age of Enlightenment
(18th century)

The Age of Enlightenment was a period where many people rejected traditional authority and embraced knowledge obtained through science and reason. This chapter will explore twenty facts about the impact that the Age of Enlightenment had on society.

506. **The Age of Enlightenment lasted from the late 17th century to the early 19th century.** It was a time when many people questioned authority and tradition, believing knowledge should be gained through reason and science instead.

507. **It started in Europe but spread around the world to places such as North America and South America.**

508. During this era, **new ideas about government, religion, science, and philosophy emerged.**

509. **Rene Descartes is often regarded as an important thinker who helped kickstart the Age of Enlightenment with his Discourse on the Method (1637).**

510. **Famous figures from this period include Voltaire, Jean-Jacques Rousseau, Benjamin Franklin, and Thomas Jefferson.** These thinkers helped shape modern society with their writings and philosophies on life.

511. **Newspapers were widely circulated during the Age of Enlightenment,** which allowed for discussions between citizens and led to changes in how governments were run across Europe.

512. **Many Enlightenment thinkers believed in religious tolerance and the freedom of speech,** seeing them as natural human rights.

513. **A lot of art was created that symbolized new values related to human rights, such as liberty or patriotism.** These included paintings like Jacques Louis David's Death of Marat (1793) and Francisco Goya's Third of May (1808).

514. New ideas about education were developed that emphasized the importance of individual learning and critical thinking skills over memorization or rote learning.

515. The Age of Enlightenment had a major influence on the American Revolution, the French Revolution, and other political upheavals in Europe during and after this period.

516. Many countries tried to adopt constitutional governments to replace monarchies, although it would take time for this to happen. The people began to believe more in a democracy than absolute power.

517. The United States of America broke away from Great Britain. It declared independence from colonial rule and set up its own set of laws based on principles from Enlightenment philosophy.

518. This era saw an increase in literacy. Books became easier to access due to cheaper printing methods.

519. The use of reason was seen as key, with many philosophers believing in the power of logical thinking and debate to answer questions about life and society.

520. The importance of reason and rational thinking were some of the values that had largely been lost after the fall of the Roman Empire.

521. Human rights started to be discussed more seriously during this period, leading to reforms such as abolishing the slave trade in some parts of Europe, though not all.

522. Coffee houses were popular among intellectuals, who would gather there to discuss ideas on politics, science, and other topics while enjoying their drinks.

523. The colony of Australia was established in 1788. Prisoners from Britain were sent there instead of being held prisoner in their home country.

524. This period saw an increase in public education, which allowed more people to have access to knowledge and learning opportunities.

525. One important philosopher was John Locke. He believed the mind was a tabula rasa (blank slate) at birth and that knowledge came from experience.

The Industrial Revolution
(18th–19th Centuries)

The Industrial Revolution marked a major turning point in human history. This section will take a closer look at this period by exploring twenty interesting facts about how people worked and lived, as well as some of the technological innovations that were discovered.

526. **The Industrial Revolution began in Britain in the late 1700s.** It was a period of new inventions and technology that made machines more powerful and faster than ever before.

527. **During the Industrial Revolution, factories were built to produce goods faster and cheaper than before.** This allowed people to buy things they previously could not afford.

528. **Coal and steam power were used to run these factories.**

529. **Thousands of jobs were created.** Many people moved from farms to cities, looking for new opportunities.

530. **Textiles like cotton and wool became big industries during this time.** Factory-made cloth replaced handspun clothing produced at home or on small looms.

531. **Innovations like the cotton gin allowed farmers to produce larger quantities of cotton much faster than before.** This drove down prices, which made clothing more widely accessible to all social classes.

532. **Railroads became an important means of transportation for both raw materials needed in industrial production processes and finished products.**

533. **New sources of energy, such as petroleum fuel oil,** enabled ships to carry goods around the world much more quickly.

534. **The development of a technique called the Bessemer process made it possible to mass-produce steel,** which was used in many new inventions and machines during this era.

535. The telegraph changed how people communicated with one another. This invention was followed by the invention of the telephone by Alexander Graham Bell.

536. The Industrial Revolution saw an increase in life expectancy, as advances in medicine increased access to better healthcare for more people.

537. Many women found new work opportunities in factories or mills. There was a lot of gender inequality at this time, and becoming a major part of the workforce led to suffrage movements.

538. Immigration rates rose significantly during this period, with millions of Europeans traveling in search of new jobs and lives. Many Europeans moved to the United States.

539. The Industrial Revolution changed the way people shopped. Stores began to offer a greater variety of goods and extended credit options for customers who could not afford upfront payments.

540. Machine tools were created that allowed for faster production times with fewer workers needed, resulting in lower labor costs that made many products affordable to more people.

541. Production processes became standardized, leading to improved quality control for mass-produced goods. Consumers knew what they were buying was reliable.

542. Gas lighting replaced candles or lamps, providing safer light sources in homes since there wasn't a risk of fire from open flames.

543. Industrialization came with a lot of drawbacks. For example, Europe saw an increase in pollution due to the burning of coal, oil, and other materials used for power generation.

544. Factory workers often had to work long hours under dangerous conditions. They received very little pay, and there were few protections in place.

545. In 1712, **James Watt invented the steam engine.** Steam power became the most popular energy source for machines and transportation.

The French Revolution
(1789–1799)

The French Revolution was one of the most tumultuous and influential periods in European history. In this chapter, we will explore thirty interesting facts about the revolution, including how it began, its significant leaders, and its impactful reforms.

546. **The French Revolution saw France change from an absolute monarchy to a republic with democratic ideals.**

547. **It began in 1787, and it would last until 1799, when Napoleon Bonaparte emerged on the scene to take control of France.**

548. **The general reasons behind the revolution included high taxes and prices,** poverty, a national economic crisis, and the struggling state of the peasant population of France.

549. **King Louis XVI was a very unpopular figure.** He lived an extremely lavish life, as did the members of the upper echelons of society, something that fueled dissent against the commoners.

550. **The revolution began when an institution called the Estates-General was summoned by the French finance minister** to deal with the economic crisis.

551. **The Estates-General was composed of the First Estate** (the clergy), **the Second Estate** (nobility), and **the Third Estate** (the commoners).

552. **The Third Estate was the largest, containing six hundred members,** while the First and Second Estates contained three hundred members each. However, each estate only got one vote each.

553. **The Third Estate wanted more power since they were the biggest group.** It declared itself a new body, the National Assembly, which threatened to proceed without the consent of the other estates.

554. **The National Assembly swore an oath not to disband before it had given France a new constitution** and forced the other members of the Estates-General to join it.

555. On July 14th, 1789, **thousands of enraged people in Paris stormed the Bastille, which was a prison fortress.** They were looking for gunpowder and weapons.

556. **The French saw the Bastille as a symbol for the monarchy's tyranny.** Bastille Day is still celebrated to this day!

557. **After storming the Bastille, revolutionaries formed their own armed force called the National Guard,** with the intention of putting up better resistance against those loyal to the throne.

558. **Popular French writers, like Voltaire, wrote satirical stories** poking fun at government officials, which helped fuel public discontentment before and during the revolution.

559. **King Louis XVI tried to flee Paris with his family to organize a counter-revolution in June of 1791,** but was arrested at the small town of Varennes northeast of the French capital.

560. **The new regime led by the National Constituent Assembly introduced a range of reforms that weakened the nobility and the church.** It redistributed lands to pay off public debt, gave new rights to lower classes, and implemented a new administrative system to better govern the country.

561. **The Declaration of the Rights of Man and of the Citizen asserted the universal values of liberty, equality, and brotherhood were essential values.**

562. **Queen Marie Antoinette, the wife of Louis XVI, was a strong opponent of the revolution.** She was also arrested after the royal family tried to flee France.

563. **Marie Antoinette is well known for saying, "Let them eat cake,"** but there is no evidence to suggest that she ever said these words.

564. **In 1792, France was dragged into a war with European powers that wished to put an end to the revolution** since it threatened the positions of absolute monarchs throughout the continent.

565. **The war ended with a French defeat,** but the monarchy was not reinstated by the foreign powers.

566. **The revolution saw many different political factions, such as the Girondins, the Montagnards, and the Jacobins,** who fought for their own versions of what the new France should look like.

567. **In 1793, both King Louis XVI and Queen Marie Antoinette were tried and executed.** They were charged with high treason.

568. **Maximilien Robespierre rose to prominence during the French Revolution.** He took harsh measures against those suspected to be against the revolution.

569. **Robespierre led his own political party called the Jacobins. They wanted equality before the law,** but they also believed strongly in executing anyone who opposed their cause.

570. **The Reign of Terror was a violent period during which hundreds of thousands of people were arrested.** Thousands died by guillotine in an effort to "purify" France. Robespierre himself was beheaded on July 28th, 1794.

571. In 1795, **a new government was formed called the Directory.** It was composed of five members that co-governed the state.

572. **After the formation of the Directory, a young general named Napoleon Bonaparte** started to rise in prominence for his military victories during a military campaign in Italy.

573. **France experienced massive cultural changes during the revolution.** It adopted a new national anthem, adopted the metric system, established public education for all citizens (including girls), and abolished slavery in its colonies.

574. **Napoleon would gain a lot of popularity and support from his own troops.** He and some followers overthrew the Directory in 1799 in the Coup of the 18 Brumaire.

575. **The coup abolished the Directory and established the new three-person Consulate, with Napoleon at its head,** leading to a new era in European history.

The Napoleonic Wars
(1803–1815)

The Napoleonic Wars were a series of battles fought between many countries in Europe. This section will explore thirty facts about this period, including the countries involved and how the conflicts impacted Europe.

576. **The Napoleonic Wars refers to a series of military campaigns fought between 1803 and 1815.** These conflicts were between France and other European states, most notably Great Britain, Austria, Russia, Prussia, Portugal, Spain, and Sweden.

577. After becoming First Consul with the Coup of 18 Brumaire, **Napoleon assumed almost total control of revolutionary France in 1799.**

578. **Upon gaining power, Napoleon implemented a range of political and economic reforms** that strengthened his position and helped France recover from the terrible events it had suffered during the French Revolution.

579. **Napoleon reorganized the French Army, introducing new recruitment and conscription laws and making it much stronger than it had been before.** He also chose to lead the army personally.

580. In 1803, **Great Britain declared war on France,** having noticed France's recent rise in power and Napoleon's declared interest in spreading the ideals of the French Revolution to the rest of Europe.

581. In October 1805, **French naval forces were crushed by the British at the Battle of Trafalgar.** This battle is well known for **the death of Horatio Nelson**, who became a British legend.

582. **Napoleon achieved a great victory against a combined Austro-Russian army at the Battle of Austerlitz** in late 1805. This battle led to the creation of **the Confederation of the Rhine,** which eventually led to the end of **the Holy Roman Empire.**

583. **The British Royal Navy was one of the most powerful navies in the world** at the time. It kept Napoleon from launching an invasion of Britain.

584. **Napoleon defeated the Austrian, Prussian, German, Swedish, and Russian coalitions** until he gained control over most of western and central Europe by 1809.

585. In 1807, **Napoleon led an invasion into Portugal, Britain's ally, and occupied Lisbon.**

586. **Napoleon deposed the Spanish king and installed his brother as the new king of Spain in 1808.**

587. **There was a widespread revolt in Iberia, where a large portion of Napoleon's forces were occupied for six years,** having to fight fierce opposition from Spanish and Portuguese guerilla fighters before their eventual defeat in 1814.

588. **Napoleon organized a blockade called the Continental System against Britain,** which limited the European states' ability to trade with the British. Napoleon wanted to weaken his rival economically.

589. In 1812, **Russia supposedly broke its pledge as a member of the Continental System. Napoleon decided to invade Russia** with an army of over 600,000 soldiers because of this and other reasons.

590. **The invasion of Russia would become his greatest mistake. The Russians never met the French in battle,** drawing them into the remote Russian heartland and razing towns and villages during their retreat.

591. **In Russia, Napoleon's army suffered terrible casualties due to the extreme cold and Russian tactics.** Only about 10 percent of Napoleon's soldiers survived the campaign.

592. **France never recovered from the Russian campaign.** Its rivals consolidated their forces once again and defeated Napoleon at Leipzig in 1813.

593. **Coalition forces, consisting of Austria, Prussia, and Russia,** captured Paris in March 1814.

594. **Napoleon was forced to abdicate. He was exiled to Elba,** an island in the Mediterranean Sea off the coast of Italy.

595. In 1815, **Napoleon escaped from exile but was finally defeated at the Battle of Waterloo by a British-led coalition led by Duke Wellington.**

596. **Some believe Napoleon could have won the battle. The heavy rains that took place made Napoleon delay his plans,** which gave the coalition time to regroup.

597. **The Battle of Waterloo is considered one of the most famous battles in European history.** It was the second-bloodiest battle that took place during the Napoleonic Wars.

598. **The Congress of Vienna (1814–1815) resulted in the formation of a new political order in Europe,** which became known as the Concert of Europe. It was meant to maintain the balance of power in the continent.

599. **The wars changed military tactics permanently.** For example, guerrilla warfare became more popular due to its effectiveness against larger armies.

600. **It is believed millions of civilians died due to war-related diseases or famine.**

601. **Many technological advancements occurred during this period.** For example, new types of muskets and artillery were developed, which allowed armies to fire more rapidly than ever before.

602. **Napoleon's efforts to spread a unified system of laws across Europe, known as the Napoleonic Code,** were crucial for individual states in establishing their own system of laws.

603. **During these wars, there was an upsurge in nationalism among European populations** that eventually led to the formation of modern nation-states, such as Italy and Germany.

604. **Napoleon's decline meant the rise of Britain.** The British consolidated their economic power and possessed the most powerful navy in the world.

605. **France lost all of the territories it gained during the wars.** Russia added much of Poland to its control, and Prussia gained lands as well.

The Greek War of Independence
(1821–1829)

The Greek War of Independence was a major event in modern history that saw Greece fight for its independence. This chapter will explore this fascinating period and look at twenty-five interesting facts about it.

606. **The Greek War of Independence was fought from 1821 to 1829.** Greek nationalists wanted to gain **independence from the Ottoman Empire** and establish a sovereign Greek state.

607. **This war was a very influential conflict that established many international precedents** and helped shape the way for future revolutionary wars against empires.

608. **A group called the Filiki Eteria** ("Society of Friends") was an important part of beginning **the revolution against the Ottomans,** who had ruled over Greece since 1453 CE.

609. **The Filiki Eteria was inspired by the French Revolution,** whose events had made it clear that people belonging to the same nation could come together to overthrow absolute rule.

610. **This group included prominent figures like Alexander Ypsilantis, Theodoros Kolokotronis, Demetrius Ypsilantis, and Georgios Karaiskakis.**

611. **The leader of the Greek Revolution was a man named Ioannis Kapodistrias,** who later became the first prime minister of Greece after independence had been achieved. He was called the governor of Greece.

612. **The revolution was planned to begin on March 25th, 1821, but the conspirators were forced to start the insurrection a month earlier** since the Ottomans found out about their plans.

613. **In February 1821, Greeks in the Peloponnese region rose up against their Ottoman rulers** and declared independence for Greece.

614. Famous intellectuals believed so strongly in the Greeks' cause. American physician Samuel Howe and English poet Lord Byron joined the revolution.

615. The first flag of independent Greece was based on an ancient symbol known as the cross-in-square, which is still used today by many Orthodox churches around the world.

616. Many countries, such as Britain and France, supported Greece during this war, but Russia became its most powerful ally.

617. These European powers sent their fleets to provide much-needed naval assistance to Greek revolutionaries who were being outmatched at sea by the Ottomans.

618. The Ottoman Empire had experienced a long period of decline, which allowed many different nationalities under its control to challenge it and fight for independence.

619. Greek revolts sparked up all around the Ottoman Empire. The Ottomans were unable to deal with all of them and were forced to reorganize their defenses.

620. The Ottoman forces were so badly organized that they suffered heavy defeats at the hands of the Greek military forces, even at sea.

621. The Ottomans requested aid from Egypt to counter the Greek victories, but international pressure rendered their efforts useless.

622. The Battle of Navarino in 1827 was a major victory for the Greeks and helped them gain international recognition from countries like Britain, Russia, and France.

623. At an assembly known as the London Protocol, Great Britain and Russia jointly recognized an independent Greece in 1830, something that was reaffirmed two years later when the Ottoman Empire accepted its defeat.

624. **Prince Otto von Wittelsbach from Bavaria was chosen by King George IV of England to become Greece's first monarch.** He did not have much success due to political unrest in Greece, which lasted until 1862, when he was deposed.

625. **Greece's national anthem is called "Hymn to Liberty,"** which was written by Dionysios Solomos in 1823.

626. **After gaining independence, Greece was made into a constitutional monarchy.** The monarchy was abolished in the late 20th century.

627. **The war saw significant advances in naval technology, such as the development of steam-powered ships,** something that helped to ensure victory at battles such as Navarino.

628. **Interestingly, Haiti, which had gained its independence from France a couple of decades earlier,** was the first nation to recognize Greece as a fully sovereign nation.

629. **The Treaty of Constantinople,** signed in 1832, defined the new borders between Greece and the Ottoman Empire.

630. **The Greek War of Independence led to other countries, such as Serbia, Bulgaria, and Romania, g**aining their independence from Ottoman rule.

The Crimean War
(1853–1856)

The Crimean War was a major international conflict that involved millions of soldiers. In this chapter, we explore twenty fascinating facts about this war, including the technologies that were used, a nurse's heroic efforts, and more!

631. **The Crimean War was fought between Russia and an alliance of countries, including Britain, France, and the Ottoman Empire.**

632. **It lasted from 1853 to 1856 and involved millions of soldiers on both sides.** They fought various battles across Europe and the Middle East.

633. **It began when Russian troops invaded the Ottoman Empire's territory of Crimea** after a disagreement about who should control it.

634. **One of the reasons behind the outbreak of the war was the alleged mistreatment of Eastern Orthodox subjects in Ottoman-controlled Palestine.**

635. **Russia demanded that the Eastern Orthodox population of the Ottoman Empire be placed under the protection of Tsar Nicholas I,** something that was rejected by the Ottoman government as it would have given Russia considerable influence.

636. **It was after this refusal that Russia decided to launch an invasion of Ottoman lands in July of 1853,** attacking Ottoman-controlled Romania.

637. **Another reason behind Russia's aggressive policy was the declining strength of the Ottoman Empire,** which put the future of Europe's balance of power established after the Napoleonic Wars into question.

638. **The allied forces won two key naval victories over Russian fleets at Sinope** (in modern-day Turkey) in November 1853 and Taganrog Bay (in modern-day Russia) in January 1855.

639. **The siege of Sevastopol, which lasted for eleven months, was the decisive turning point for the war.** The allied forces managed to defeat the Russians after very intense fighting.

640. **Russia sued for peace after the defeat at Sevastopol,** fearing that its heartland would be invaded by the allied forces.

641. **The conflict ended with a victory for Britain, France,** and the Ottoman Empire. Russia had to give up some of its lands near Crimea with **the Treaty of Paris of 1856.**

642. **The British and French supported the Ottomans because they feared the empire would have been decisively defeated by the Russians,** which would upset the balance of power in Europe.

643. **Diseases like cholera and typhus killed more soldiers during the Crimean War than fighting did.**

644. **The war saw one of the first uses of photography to document battles and conditions on battlefields as battles unfolded,** helping people back home understand what was happening in real time.

645. **The Crimean War is sometimes referred to as the first "modern" war.**

646. **Lord Aberdeen, the prime minister of the United Kingdom, resigned soon after the Treaty of Paris was signed.** The public was upset about the mismanagement and high cost of the war.

647. **Many paintings depicting scenes from the Crimean War became popular across Europe,** such as William Simpson's painting Charge of the Heavy Brigade at Balaklava.

648. **Florence Nightingale, a famous English nurse, set up field hospitals and trained nurses at Scutari Hospital near Istanbul,** where she treated wounded soldiers and used improved sanitation practices.

649. **The Crimean War greatly weakened the Russian army.** It would take decades for Russia to recover.

650. **Leo Tolstoy, the famous Russian author who wrote War and Peace, served during the Crimean War.**

The Revolutions of 1848

This chapter will explore the fascinating history of the revolutions of 1848 by taking a look at twenty interesting facts about this period. Why did they start? Were any reforms made because of them? Through these facts, we'll be able to gain an understanding of why this period was so significant for many European countries!

651. **The revolutions of 1848 were a series of uprisings that happened in many countries in Europe** in the mid-19th century.

652. **This period is often called the Springtime of Nations due to its widespread nature,** prominence of nationalist sentiments, and hope for positive outcomes.

653. **The revolutions began in France, where people demanded more freedom and democracy from the government.**

654. **During the June Days, barricades were built by protestors on the streets of Paris.** They were protesting proposed reforms by the government.

655. **The French police brutally suppressed the protesters,** resulting in about ten thousand casualties and thousands of deportations.

656. **Inspired by the events in France, people across Europe protested against their rulers** to gain more rights and be represented more fairly in government.

657. **The revolutions spread quickly to other countries, including Austria, Prussia (now Germany), Italy, and Hungary.**

658. **In Vienna, there was an uprising called the March Revolution,** with university students leading a march through the city and demanding reform.

659. **The revolutions of 1848 were a turning point for Europe,** as it was the first time popular movements had come together to fight for change in multiple countries.

660. **The results of the revolutions varied from place to place, but on the whole,** the intended outcomes of establishing liberal governments or nation-states were unsuccessful.

661. In some places, **like France, protests led to the adoption of a new constitution,** which guaranteed some new rights.

662. **The small German states demanded German unification. While this was not achieved in 1848,** it fueled sentiment that would last until German unification in 1871.

663. **Italy saw some reforms, including abolishing censorship of books and newspapers,** which helped spread more information among citizens.

664. **In the Austrian Empire, which contained people from many different nations,** the revolution posed a great threat to Habsburg rule.

665. **With the help of Russian military intervention, the Habsburgs were able to brutally suppress the revolutionaries.** The revolutionaries achieved limited progress toward liberalism.

666. **Hungary declared itself independent from Austrian rule. Lajos Kossuth became its leader** and introduced many reforms, such as abolishing feudalism and granting land to the peasantry.

667. **The revolutions of 1848 sparked a wave of migration from Europe to North America,** leading to one of the largest migrant waves in American history.

668. **Writers like Victor Hugo wrote about these revolutions at the time,** which helped spread awareness among citizens.

669. **Karl Marx and Friedrich Engels famously wrote The Communist Manifesto in 1848, outlining their vision for a communist society.** Marx was involved in the German revolution of 1848.

670. **Although many of the revolutions during the Springtime of Nations would fail to achieve their intended outcomes, they would spark a broader sense of liberal nationalism throughout the continent.** The revolutions led to very influential developments, such as the formation of countries as we know them today.

The Unification of Germany
(1871)

This chapter will explore the historic unification of Germany in 1871. We'll take a look at twenty-five interesting facts about how separate German-speaking states joined together to form one country and the role played by Otto von Bismarck.

671. **The unification of Germany happened in 1871 when German-speaking states joined to form one country called Germany.**

672. **Ever since the dawn of the Holy Roman Empire,** the territory of modern-day Germany was divided between hundreds of smaller states, baronies, duchies, and city-states.

673. **These political entities, for the most part, all shared a common German culture and language,** but the complex political dynamics and structures within the Holy Roman Empire had made it nearly impossible to form a united German state.

674. **This changed after the Napoleonic Wars.** Napoleon defeated and reorganized the German states, abolishing the Holy Roman Empire.

675. **By the time of Germany's unification in 1871, there were still up to forty independent German states, with the Kingdom of Prussia,** located in the north, being the largest.

676. **In almost all of the German states, revolutionary and nationalist sentiments were expressed during the Springtime of Nations,** so the spirit for unification was high by the time the process began.

677. **The unification process was led by Prussian Chancellor Otto von Bismarck,** an excellent diplomat who realized that the possibility of German unification under Prussia was possible.

678. **A major opponent of Bismarck and Prussia was the Habsburg Austrian Empire, which also spoke German and shared the German culture.** The Austrian Empire had economic and political interests in unifying the smaller German states.

679. In 1834, **the German states were united in an economic union, the Zollverein, which was led by Prussia.**

680. **At the beginning of the 1860s, Bismarck realized that Austria had been weakened by its recent defeat in a war against France and the Kingdom of Piedmont.** He knew that it was time to start the process of unification.

681. **Otto von Bismarck famously declared in a speech in 1862,** "The great questions of the time will not be resolved by speeches and majority decisions ... but by iron and blood." This statement reflected his belief in the importance of military power in achieving German unity.

682. **In 1866, Prussia and Austria went to war over a German province on the border with Denmark named Holstein. Austria' was defeated in just over six weeks.**

683. **The first official leader of a united Germany was Kaiser Wilhelm I,** who came from Prussia's royal family, the Hohenzollern dynasty.

684. **In 1866, Prussia proclaimed the creation of the North German Confederation,** which it would lead.

685. **The North German Confederation adopted the North German Constitution,** which made it a constitutional monarchy based on federalism.

686. From 1866 to 1871, **Bismarck initiated domestic policies that served to strengthen local production and stimulate economic growth.** He also retrained the military.

687. **In 1870, Prussia, with the support of the North German Confederation,** went to war with France. France was seen as the new main rival after Austria's defeat.

688. The Franco-Prussian War of 1870–1871 played a crucial role in the unification of Germany, with the Prussians able to achieve a decisive victory that had been largely unexpected.

689. At the Palace of Versailles, the German Empire, or the German Reich, was officially proclaimed on January 18th, 1871, with Kaiser Wilhelm I becoming its first emperor.

690. Prussia's victory over France weakened French influence in Europe and helped to rally support for German nationalism and accelerate the process of unification.

691. After reunification, Berlin became the capital city of Germany. It still is today.

692. A strong sense of nationalism has been associated with Germany, and its citizens are proud to call themselves Germans regardless of their regional origin or background.

693. German unification inspired many similar movements in Europe, most notably the unification of Italy, which took place around the same time.

694. The unification of Germany and its strong military created a new European superpower. Germany became one of the most dominant nations in the continent.

695. Thanks to Bismarck's talents as a diplomat, the German Empire experienced marvelous economic growth that was directed to maintaining a professional army and the new balance of power in Europe.

The Unification of Italy
(1871)

This chapter explores the Italian unification, a movement that saw many states unified into one country. We'll take a look at twenty-five interesting facts about how this was achieved, from key figures to revolts.

696. **The unification of Italy would conclude in 1871,** although the Italians' journey for unification began way back in 1848.

697. Much like Germany, **the Italian Peninsula in the 19th century was made up of smaller states** that largely shared a common culture.

698. **With the spread of liberal and nationalist ideas in the 19th century,** the Risorgimento movement was formed, which sought to unify the Italian nation.

699. **By the time the unification process began in the 1840s, the south of Italy was controlled by the Kingdom of the Two Sicilies,** the central territories were controlled by the Papal States, and the north of the peninsula was contested by several states, including **the Kingdom of Sardinia-Piedmont, the Duchy of Tuscany, and the Austrian-controlled Kingdom of Lombardy-Venetia.**

700. **The Carbonari group was crucial in Italian unification.** It had been created as a secret political organization in the early 19th century and pushed for Italian nationalism and independence from French and Habsburg influence.

701. **Two of the Carbonari leaders were Giuseppe Mazzini and Giuseppe Garibaldi.** They played important roles in Italian unification.

702. **Garibaldi was from Piedmont and escaped prison in 1834. He went to South America,** where he gained a lot of practice participating in Latin American revolutionary wars. He mastered the art of guerilla warfare and would return to Italy in 1848.

703. **Mazzini was the statesman of the Carbonari.** He was arrested a couple of times for revolutionary activities.

704. **The Kingdom of Sardinia-Piedmont would lead the process of Italian unification.**

705. In 1848, **during the First Italian War of Independence, the Kingdom of Sardinia-Piedmont went to war with Habsburg Austria.**

706. **Piedmont had the help of local revolutionaries.** They wanted to end conservative rule in Italian provinces controlled by Austria.

707. **During the same year, there would be a liberal revolt against the Bourbon monarchy in the Kingdom of the Two Sicilies,** which would be suppressed by the king.

708. **The First Italian War of Independence ended in an Austrian victory.** France intervened to restore the status quo and keep Italy disintegrated.

709. **Prime Minister Camillo Cavour eventually created an alliance between Sardinia-Piedmont and France against Habsburg Austria.** The two sides would go to war in 1859 during the Second War of Italian Independence.

710. **This time, the French and the Sardinians emerged victorious,** forcing Austria to cede control of the provinces of Lombardy, Modena, and Emilia.

711. **One year later, Giuseppe Garibaldi led a secret military expedition to overthrow the Sicilian monarchy and annex southern Italian provinces to the Kingdom of Sardinia-Piedmont.**

712. **The Expedition of the Thousand managed to liberate Sicily and overthrow the Sicilian monarchy.** The revolutionaries also took most of the Papal States' territories in central Italy.

713. In 1861, **the Kingdom of the Two Sicilies was annexed by united Italy following a referendum that saw 97 percent of Sicilians vote for unifying with Italy.**

714. **The united Kingdom of Italy was officially proclaimed in March 1861,** with the title of king assumed by Victor Emmanuel II of Sardinia.

715. In 1866, the Kingdom of Italy, which controlled most of the Italian Peninsula, joined Prussia in defeating Austria.

716. During the war, the Kingdom of Italy claimed the Austrian Italian territories of Veneto, Friuli, and Mantua.

717. The unification of Italy would be completed in 1871 with the annexation of Rome after a German victory in the Franco-Prussian War.

718. Pope Pius IX opposed unification, something that led to the Papal States being annexed by Italy following the capture of Rome in 1870, ending papal rule in Italy.

719. Rome became the capital city after it was incorporated into Italy.

720. After unification took place, there were more investments in infrastructure, which led to improvements in industrialization, railway networks, and education systems.

721. Unification helped shape modern Italy and its culture as we know it today, including music, art, and literature.

722. Italian unification was a long and difficult process that took many decades to complete, unlike German unification, which was achieved in the span of about fifteen years.

723. Prime Minister Camillo Cavour passed away shortly after unification had taken place. His efforts are still remembered today for helping to create modern-day Italy.

724. The national anthem of Italy, "Il Canto degli Italiani," was composed in 1847 during the height of nationalist sentiment. It is the country's national anthem today.

725. The design for the modern national flag of Italy was adopted during Italy's

unification. The tricolor flag was used by **Sardinian Carbonari** and later spread all around the nation.

The Scramble for Africa and Bismarck's Europe
(1871–1914)

The Scramble for Africa, which took place primarily during the late 19th and early 20th centuries, was a period of intense colonization and imperial expansion by European powers across **the African continent.** This era also saw **the rise of Prussia.** These thirty interesting facts will shed light on this formative period in European history.

726. **The last three decades of the 19th century and the first decade of the 20th century** saw a series of political maneuvers in Europe that culminated with the outbreak of World War I.

727. **With the unification of Italy and Germany, two new powerful empires had been created in Europe.** They were in competition with the already strong French, British, Russian, and Austrian superpowers.

728. **To maintain the balance of power between these large empires and prevent the outbreak of a major conflict, Otto von Bismarck** believed it was necessary to contain France, which had run over all of **Europe during Napoleon's reign.**

729. **In 1879, Germany entered a defensive alliance with Austria-Hungary. Italy joined in 1882, making it the Triple Alliance.**

730. **All three states agreed to secret arrangements and pledged to follow each other in a conflict against France.**

731. France gathered its own allies. **Its main ally was the declining Russian Empire.**

732. **France and Russia signed an agreement in 1891 and had an alliance three years later.** The French lent the Russians a lot of funds to rebuild and modernize their infrastructure and military.

733. **Germany increased its military and economy to the point that it seriously challenged Great Britain,** which had emerged as the de facto hegemon of 19th-century Europe.

734. **Great Britain had the strongest navy, an extensive system of colonies, a powerful military, and a large economy.** It also enjoyed an isolated policy, so it was not as affected by the politics of continental Europe.

735. **With Germany's rise to prominence, British foreign policy changed,** with the nation signing agreements with France and Russia.

736. **Britain, Russia, and France formed the Triple Entente to balance against the Triple Alliance.**

737. **The Berlin Conference (1884–1885) saw all of the major powers of Europe come to the negotiating table to discuss the future of Europe** and the rest of the world.

738. **It kicked off the Scramble for Africa, a race to claim lands and colonize Africa,** which was still largely unexplored by Europeans at that time.

739. **The Berlin Conference did not involve drawing arbitrary borders on a map of Africa. Instead,** it formalized existing colonial claims and sought to establish guidelines for future territorial acquisitions.

740. **At the start of the Scramble for Africa, only 10 percent of African land had been claimed by Europeans.** By 1900, that figure had risen to 90 percent.

741. **Many African tribes were forced out or enslaved during this period,** leading to significant loss of life on both sides due to wars fought over territories.

742. **European colonists brought their own culture, language, religion, laws, and education system** into the regions they occupied, replacing the traditional ways of doing things.

743. France was very active during this period. It acquired more land than any other European nation in West Africa.

744. Great Britain was the dominant power in southern Africa. It acquired colonies in Nigeria, Sudan, Uganda, and Kenya.

745. Portugal established its colony in Angola, and Italy took control of Libya.

746. Germany was late to enter the Scramble for Africa, but it acquired Togoland (now part of Ghana), Cameroon, and German East Africa (Rwanda and Burundi).

747. The European empires justified their ruthless conquest and colonization of the African continent with the belief they were brining enlightenment and progress to the uncivilized parts of the world.

748. **Millions of Africans suffered under brutal colonial rule.** Many were forced to move from their homes, and they experienced terrible living conditions.

749. **The Scramble for Africa led to economic suffering,** as Britain and other countries took resources from colonies with no intention of providing fair trading opportunities.

750. **This period saw the rise of nationalistic feelings among people all over the continent who wanted freedom from colonial rule.** Several independence movements took place after WWI.

751. **Many African countries still suffer from economic inequality and political unrest.** Many political scholars believe this is because of the Scramble for Africa.

752. **The Scramble for Africa shaped much of the current international law governing relations between different states** regarding issues like land rights and resource extraction.

753. **The Scramble for Africa stimulated rivalries between European superpowers,** especially between Germany, France, and Britain.

754. **The British-German rivalry would lead to a naval arms race,** with the newly created German navy challenging the supremacy of **the British Royal Navy** by 1914.

755. **Austria-Hungary slowly absorbed the Balkan nation-states,** which would try to gain their independence from the crumbling Ottoman Empire.

The Balkan Wars
(1912–1913)

The Balkan Wars were a pivotal period in the history of southeastern Europe. Let's unpack twenty facts about how these conflicts began and their impact on World War I.

756. **The Balkan Wars were two conflicts fought between 1912 and 1913.** They resulted in the emergence of new Balkan states and the weakening of the Ottoman Empire.

757. **The First Balkan War occurred from October 1912 to May 1913 and involved the Balkan League** (Serbia, Montenegro, Greece, and Bulgaria) **against the Ottoman Empire.**

758. **The main objective of the Balkan League was to expel the Ottoman Empire from the Balkans** and to gain territory in the region where these nationalities had lived for centuries under Ottoman suzerainty.

759. **The Balkan League quickly achieved significant victories against the Ottoman Empire,** capturing territories in present-day Albania, Macedonia, and Thrace.

760. **The Battle of Kumanovo in October 1912 resulted in a decisive victory for the Balkan League against the Ottomans in Macedonia.**

761. **The Siege of Adrianople (Edirne) in November 1912 was a significant military operation by Bulgarian and Serbian forces,** resulting in the capture of the city from the Ottomans.

762. **The Treaty of London was signed on May 30th, 1913,** ending the First Balkan War and recognizing significant territorial gains for the Balkan League states at the expense of **the Ottoman Empire.**

763. **It was brokered by the great powers of Europe to prevent further escalation of the conflict** and maintain stability in the region.

764. **The First Balkan War also resulted in the creation of an independent Albania.**

765. **The Second Balkan War** occurred from June to August 1913 and **involved Bulgaria against its former allies, Serbia, Greece, and Romania.**

766. **The main cause of the Second Balkan War was Bulgaria's dissatisfaction with the territorial gains it achieved in the Treaty of London.** The Bulgarians had hoped to achieve more from the first conflict.

767. **Bulgaria initiated hostilities against its former allies by attacking Serbian and Greek positions in Macedonia** in June 1913.

768. However, **the Serbian army, with support from Greece and Romania, launched a successful counteroffensive against Bulgaria,** pushing Bulgarian forces back.

769. **The Battle of Kresna Gorge in July 1913 was a significant engagement where Serbian and Greek forces defeated Bulgarian forces** attempting to advance into Greek territory.

770. **Bulgaria was forced to surrender, signing the Treaty of Bucharest on August 10th,** 1913, ending the Second Balkan War. Bulgaria suffered territorial losses.

771. **The territorial adjustments made in the Treaty of Bucharest included Serbia gaining territory in much of Macedonia,** Greece gaining southern Macedonia, and Romania gaining southern Dobruja.

772. **The Balkan Wars were very important in the context of 20th-century Europe. The conflicts significantly weakened the Ottoman Empire's presence in the Balkans,** paving the way for its eventual collapse during World War I.

773. **The Balkan Wars contributed to the growth of nationalist sentiments among various ethnic groups in the region,** leading to further conflicts and tensions in the following decades.

774. **The Balkan Wars resulted in significant population movements,** including the displacement of Muslim populations from territories captured by **the Balkan League states.**

775. **These conflicts are often seen as a prelude to World War I,** as they highlighted the complex web of alliances and rivalries in Europe.

World War I
(1914–1918)

This chapter will explore the events and facts surrounding World War I. We'll look at thirty interesting facts about how it started, the major participants, and major battles. Discover how WWI changed history forever!

776. The war began on July 28th, 1914, when **Austria declared war against Serbia in response to the assassination of Archduke Franz Ferdinand.**

777. **Archduke Franz Ferdinand and his wife were assassinated during their visit to the Bosnian city of Sarajevo by Serbian nationalist Gavrilo Princip.**

778. **Serbs, Bosnians, Croats, and other Balkan peoples who had been under the conservative rulership of the Austro-Hungarian Empire were discontent with Habsburg rule.** They wanted independence, and some went to extremes to achieve their goals.

779. **The assassination of Archduke Franz Ferdinand was followed by a series of diplomatic maneuvers by European nations.** This period was known as **the July Crisis,** during which time European countries mobilized their forces and prepared for war.

780. **Russia came in to defend Serbia, causing Austria to declare war on Russia,** which dragged in France, Germany, and Great Britain.

781. **World War I would be the largest war fought by any state at that point in history.**

782. **The total number of casualties was around forty million.** There were around twenty million deaths and twenty-one million wounded. This number includes both civilians and military personnel.

783. **The Ottoman Empire joined the war in 1915 on the side of the Central Powers** (Germany and Austria-Hungary). **The Ottomans** wanted to save their declining empire and take control of territories in the Balkans and the Caucasus.

784. Italy and the United States sided with the Entente. Bulgaria joined the war on the side of the Central Powers.

785. World War I would be so destructive because of the implementation of new tactics and military technologies, like tanks, airplanes, and machine guns.

786. World War I became infamous for trench warfare. Soldiers would dig trench systems on the battlefield, leading to well-fortified defensive positions that would be extremely costly for the other side to attack.

787. Poison gas was used for the first time in WWI. By the end of the conflict, more than 125,000 tons of poisonous gases had been released into trenches.

788. On the Western Front, where Germany fought the British and French, the largest battles took place at the Somme and Verdun, resulting in more than 1.5 million casualties.

789. The Battle of Verdun lasted for three hundred days! It was known as the bloodiest battle in WWI, as there were more than 300,000 French and German losses.

790. After initial German advances in 1914 and 1915, the French and the British contained the German invasion, leading to a stalemate that would be broken in 1917 with the arrival of American soldiers.

791. On December 25th, 1914, British and German soldiers declared a temporary ceasefire. They exchanged gifts with each other and played a game of football. This day is known as the Christmas Truce.

792. On the Eastern Front, the German and Austrian forces pushed back the Russian soldiers, leading to and chaos in Russia.

793. The Russian Revolution in 1917 saw Russia exit the war. The revolutionaries also overthrew the Russian Empire.

794. **In 1915, the Allies launched a naval invasion of the Ottoman Empire.** They landed on the Gallipoli Peninsula, hoping to take Constantinople.

795. **The Gallipoli Campaign would last for ten months and result in about 500,000 casualties by mid-1916.** The Allies were unable to break through the Ottoman defenses.

796. **After Italy's entry into the war, the Italians tried to break through into Austria but were met with fierce resistance from Austro-German** forces in modern-day Slovenia on the Isonzo River.

797. **There would be twelve battles along the Isonzo River.** The Italians were pushed from the river in October 1917.

798. **The United States joined WWI in 1917 after German U-boats sunk several American merchant ships** carrying supplies for Allied forces without any warning or prior notice.

799. **Germany was the only Central Power that had an abundance of resources and a competent military throughout most of the war.** The Austrian, Ottoman, and Bulgarian troops lacked discipline and equipment.

800. **As the war dragged on, public sentiment in Berlin and other major German cities** made it impossible to continue the war effort.

801. **The war officially ended with the signing of the Treaty of Versailles on June 28th, 1919.** The treaty placed severe restrictions on Germany for starting the war, including heavy reparations.

802. **Other separate treaties would be signed by the defeated powers in addition to the Treaty of Versailles.**

803. **World War I marked the end of old-fashioned empires in Europe, as Germany, Austria-Hungary, and the Ottoman Empire were reorganized into new states.** The Russian Revolution put an end to the Russian Empire.

804. **The war led to the formation of multiple new nation-states around Europe, such as Czechoslovakia, Hungary, Poland, Ukraine, Georgia, Yugoslavia, and Romania,** where mostly liberal democratic regimes were established.

805. **American President Woodrow Wilson wanted to avoid the breakout of another massive war.** He helped create an international organization called the League of Nations, which many European nations joined.

The Russian Revolution and the Formation of the USSR (1917)

The Russian Revolution was a major event that greatly impacted Europe. These twenty-five fascinating facts will give you a glimpse into what led to the revolution in the first place and the figures who were involved in overthrowing the Russian Empire.

806. **The Russian Revolution began in 1917 amidst World War I** after a series of protests and worker strikes in St. Petersburg and Moscow.

807. **The lower classes dealt with poor living conditions and did not have fundamental rights or economic prosperity.** The protests also began because the Russian forces suffered several defeats in World War I.

808. **As a result of the revolution, the Russian monarch, Tsar Nicholas II,** was forced to abdicate, ending a long line of monarchic succession.

809. **Russia was reorganized into the first communist state in world history.**

810. **The first protests began in March and led to the creation of a provisional government led by the Russian Duma** (the parliamentary body).

811. Local soviets, **socialist workers' councils that governed the affairs of small districts, were also created.**

812. **A group of far-left revolutionaries known as the Bolsheviks grew increasingly influential.** They were led by Vladimir Lenin, an advocate of Marxist principles who believed that communism should be established in Russia.

813. **The Bolsheviks united the local soviets into voluntary armed militias and took control from the provisional government in October.** They established their own government: the Russian Soviet Federative Socialist Republic.

814. **Lenin was supported by Leon Trotsky, who was considered the second in command during the Russian Revolution.** He would be assassinated in 1940 while in exile in Mexico.

815. **A popular Bolshevik slogan during the revolution was "Peace, land, and bread."**

816. **The Bolsheviks signed a peace agreement with the Germans** in March 1918, exiting WWI.

817. **They implemented a range of policies that were aimed at redistributing land and resources from the wealthy to the poor.**

818. **The Bolsheviks were not unopposed.** Anti-socialist and conservative Russians united against the Bolsheviks, forming **the White Army and beginning the Russian Civil War.**

819. **The Russian Civil War ended in 1923 with the defeat of the Whites and the establishment of a socialist regime in Russia.**

820. After the victory, **the Bolsheviks reorganized themselves into the Communist Party** and continued pushing the communist agenda.

821. **The Communists started to believe they had to spread communism to the rest of the world.** They began to invade many neighboring states, including Ukraine, Moldova, and Georgia, all of which were occupied by the Red Army by 1921.

822. **Russia established the Union of Soviet Socialist Republics** (USSR) in December 1922.

823. **Communist regimes were established in newly occupied states,** and the USSR eventually grew to include fifteen members.

824. **The Communist Party took control of all aspects of society after Lenin's death in 1924,** including factories, farms, and schools. It created a one-party state where it held absolute power over the citizens.

825. **After Lenin's death, a young Communist by the name of Joseph Stalin came to power as the head of the Communist Party and the USSR.** He enforced several radical policies like the collectivization of agriculture, which resulted in millions of deaths due to starvation.

826. **Stalin pushed the one-party rule to a new level.** He began a reign of terror and imprisoned and executed hundreds of thousands who were suspected of being the state's enemies.

827. **Prisoners were forced to work in extreme conditions in hundreds of secret labor camps that were scattered around the USSR.** These prisons were known as gulags.

828. **The Soviet Union's new factories greatly increased domestic production,** though it was mostly weapons.

829. **Strict censorship of all aspects of life was implemented. Newspapers, music, theater, and art** had to go through state channels before being disseminated to the public.

830. **The USSR would push for the spread of communism around the world for decades,** financing many far-left movements in Europe and Asia.

The Interwar Period
(1918–1939)

The interwar period was a transformative time in history when the United States rose as the greatest power in the world. Technology advanced dramatically, and popular culture flourished. Let's examine these changes with thirty interesting facts.

831. **The interwar period refers to the time between World War I and World War II.**

832. **Although this period only lasted for about two decades,** the world underwent dramatic technological, socioeconomic, and political changes.

833. **After the end of WWI, democratic regimes were established throughout Europe,** with the war's victors hoping that conservative monarchies would never return to the continent.

834. **The 1920s were a time of recovery for Europe and the rest of the world.** New European nation-states were still getting their acts together and trying to find their place in the new political world order.

835. **For the most part, this decade was peaceful, with the exception of Soviet expansion** into the Caucasus and the establishment of Soviet republics in Georgia, Armenia, and Azerbaijan.

836. **Technology improved dramatically during this time.** Airplanes became much more powerful and were used more by governments around the world for military purposes or transportation reasons.

837. **Popular culture flourished during this time. Jazz music spread across Europe, and Hollywood films were seen around the globe.**

838. **Artistic movements like Surrealism, Dadaism, and Bauhaus emerged, challenging traditional notions of art and culture** and pushing boundaries in painting, sculpture, literature, and design.

839. **Radio broadcasts allowed people to listen to the news as it happened anywhere in the world!**

840. **Women gained more rights during the interwar period;** some countries even gave women the right to vote for the first time in history.

841. **The League of Nations was founded at this time.** Its purpose was to promote international peace and cooperation among nations.

842. **Despite its noble goals, the League of Nations would fail to become a strong,** respected international organization due to the emergence of new regimes that defied its laws.

843. **By the end of the 1920s, Europe and the rest of the world entered a period of great economic decline called the Great Depression.** It began in 1929 and lasted until the late 1930s. It was one of the worst economic downturns ever recorded and caused major social upheaval all over the world.

844. **Every European nation experienced effects from the Great Depression,** such as severe hyperinflation and high unemployment rates, which led to political instability.

845. **Partially as a response to the economic crisis caused by the Great Depression,** far-right nationalist leaders started to gain traction in Europe.

846. **The first prominent far-right movement was Italian fascism.** This movement was led by a former journalist turned radical politician named Benito Mussolini, who became the prime minister in 1922.

847. **Mussolini and his followers advocated for a strong Italy,** and they were ready to use violence against groups they opposed, like liberals or socialists.

848. **Similar developments took place in Germany,** which was renamed the Weimar Republic.

849. **Germany was hit the hardest by the Great Depression,** so public sentiment for revanchism (revenge) was very strong.

850. **Adolf Hitler, inspired by Mussolini's success in Italy,** came to power in 1933 and soon emerged as the dictator of Germany.

851. **His National Socialist German Workers' Party** (the Nazi Party) celebrated the superiority of the German race and stressed the importance of German rearmament and the glory of the German nation.

852. During the 1930s, **Hitler was successful in annexing Austrian and Czechoslovakian territories.** The leaders of democratic regimes in France and Great Britain reluctantly allowed aggressive German expansion.

853. **Italy and Germany formed the Axis, spreading far-right propaganda, usurping all power in the countries,** overpowering the rule of law, and investing heavily in remilitarization.

854. **Fascism became a powerful ideology,** with its proponents pushing for totalitarian control over all aspects of the state and inspiring similar movements all throughout the world.

855. **Fascism would lead to the breakout of the Spanish Civil War** (1936–1939) between those favoring a republic and those wanting a dictatorship.

856. **The Spanish Civil War ended in a victory for the Spanish fascists, who received a lot of help from Italians and Germans.** Francisco Franco would emerge as the dictator of Spain.

857. **The Soviet Union underwent radical changes under the leadership of Joseph Stalin,** who pushed for economic and social reforms.

858. **Stalin's policies were much like those of his totalitarian colleagues in Italy and Germany.** The majority of the Soviet Union's population struggled to overcome poverty and obtain basic living conditions.

859. **Several major international conferences took place during this period, including the Washington Naval Conference** (1921–1922), which sought to limit global armament levels. The Geneva Disarmament Conference (1932–1934) was aimed at reducing military spending by countries.

860. **Although the Soviets and Nazis claimed to be each other's enemies,** the two would agree to a secret plan to invade Poland together in August 1939.

World War II
(1939–1945)

From the Battle of Britain to the bombing of Hiroshima and Nagasaki, World War II was one of the most devastating conflicts in human history. In this chapter, we will explore thirty interesting facts about this influential war.

861. **World War II was the deadliest conflict in human history to date,** with around seventy-five million people killed worldwide.

862. **It started on September 1st, 1939, when Nazi Germany invaded Poland. France and the United Kingdom declared war on Germany in response.**

863. The two main factions in the war would be **the Axis (Germany, Italy and Japan)** and **the Allies (Britain, France, China, the USSR, and the US).**

864. **Germany invaded and defeated Norway and Denmark in 1940.** The Germans also launched an invasion of France through Belgium, the Netherlands, and Luxembourg.

865. **The Nazis occupied Paris on June 14th, 1940, not one year after the beginning of the war.** France signed an armistice with Germany, and the country was organized into occupation zones controlled by the Germans and the Italians.

866. **Great Britain, led by Prime Minister Winston Churchill, organized an amazing defense of the English Channel to stop the Germans from crossing and invading Britain.**

867. **The Battle of Britain was a significant air battle between the German Luftwaffe and the British Royal Air Force in 1940 over control of UK airspace.** Most major British cities, including London, were ruthlessly bombed.

868. **Hitler prepared and launched Operation Barbarossa,** which was intended to be a quick offensive against the Soviet Union in June 1941.

869. **The Soviet military was unable to respond effectively in time.** The Germans made great headway into the Soviet territories and took control of Ukraine, Belarus, and western Russia very quickly.

870. **The Soviets were able to mobilize in time to defend Moscow and Leningrad.** The Germans had to halt their invasion after exhausting their resources.

871. **Japan attacked Pearl Harbor on December 7th, 1941,** bringing **the United States officially into World War II on the side of the Allies.**

872. **The Battle of Stalingrad** (1942–1943) **saw some of the most brutal fighting during WWII.** It was a major turning point, as Nazis started to be pushed back from the Eastern Front.

873. **By the end of 1943, the German offensive into the Soviet Union had been completely halted.** The Germans organized a tactical retreat the following year after a renewed Soviet offensive.

874. **D-Day** (June 6th, 1944) **marked the beginning of the Allied victory in Europe,** with around 160,000 troops landing on five beaches in Normandy, France, to fight the Nazis.

875. **The Allies were not only successful in Normandy but also managed to launch an invasion of Italy from the Mediterranean** in 1943, taking most of southern Italy.

876. **The Allies and the Soviets closed in from the West and the East,** taking Berlin in the spring of 1945.

877. On April 30th, 1945, **Hitler committed suicide in his bunker before Allied troops could find him.**

878. **The Japanese would surrender in the autumn of 1945 after the US dropped two atomic bombs on Hiroshima and Nagasaki,** killing hundreds of thousands at once.

879. **Scientists from Europe, primarily from the United Kingdom, were involved in the Manhattan Project,** which developed the atomic bomb.

880. **When the Allies advanced into German territories, they unraveled the terrible truth the Nazis** had been hiding from the outside world: the mass murder, deportation, and imprisonment of Jews and other minorities.

881. **The Nazis organized forced labor camps in which millions of innocents perished in one of the most tragic events in history.** This event is known as the Holocaust.

882. **The genocide was justified as being part of the "Final Solution,"** which sought to establish the cultural and social dominance of the Aryan race at the expense of inferior races.

883. **The tragedy of the Holocaust is remembered thanks to the accounts of those who lived during it, like Anne Frank, who wrote her diary while hiding from Nazis during WWII.** Her diary became an iconic nonfiction book that teaches us about the horrors inflicted upon innocent people due to war and prejudice.

884. **Women worldwide took on roles as nurses, pilots,** or factory workers for their respective countries since many men were away fighting.

885. **WWII saw some major advances in technology,** including jet aircraft, radar, computers, and atomic weapons, which changed warfare forever.

886. **Bletchley Park, a country estate in England, was the site of a top-secret codebreaking operation during World War II.** The team of **codebreakers**, which included **Alan Turing,** played a crucial role in deciphering **German Enigma machine codes.**

887. **Poland's capital, Warsaw, was completely destroyed during the war.**

888. **Winston Churchill was the prime minister of the United Kingdom during WWII.** He is remembered as one of the greatest leaders in history. He helped lead his country to victory against Nazi Germany through his inspirational speeches and strategy-planning skills.

889. **The United Nations (UN) replaced the League of Nations as a global peacekeeping organization after WWII ended.** Its goal was the prevention of another large-scale war and the establishment of a new world order.

890. **Stalin occupied most of Eastern Europe and established communist regimes in countries like Poland, Romania, Czechoslovakia, and East Germany.**

The Cold War
(1945–1991)

From 1945 to 1991, the world witnessed an intense rivalry between two superpowers: the United States and the Soviet Union. Known as the **"Cold War,"** this period was characterized by a race for political influence in Europe, Asia, and Africa. In this chapter, we will explore twenty interesting facts about **the Cold War.**

891. **The Cold War was a time of tension between the United States and the Soviet Union** that lasted from 1945 to 1991.

892. **Both countries wanted to be the most powerful and spread their ideologies around the world,** which led to competition for political influence in places like Europe, Asia, and Africa.

893. **The Cold War led to a huge arms race where both powers built up their military arsenals** in an attempt to gain superiority over each other.

894. **Each side developed nuclear weapons during this period** as a deterrent against attack by the other side, but these were never used in combat.

895. **Instead of fighting directly with each other, they fought proxy wars, like in Vietnam or Korea,** where both sides supported different sides in a conflict without actually entering into direct battle themselves.

896. **Throughout the Cold War, Eastern European states were under heavy Soviet influence.** Puppet communist regimes spread anti-Western propaganda and limited the freedoms of their citizens.

897. In March 1946, **Winston Churchill said in a speech that an Iron Curtain had descended upon Europe,** symbolizing the split between democratic and communist European states.

898. **This rivalry led to space exploration. Each country competed for superiority in technology and science.** Russia launched **Sputnik 1,** the first artificial satellite ever sent into orbit.

899. From 1948 to 1949, **the Soviet Union blockaded West Berlin, cutting off all land and water routes to the city.** In response, the West organized the Berlin Airlift, a massive airlift operation to supply West Berlin with food, fuel, and other essentials. The airlift lasted for eleven months.

900. **The Cold War saw huge growth in international organizations like NATO and the United Nations,** which were formed to prevent future wars.

901. **Important documents, such as the Helsinki Accords, were signed during this time,** outlining agreements on how different countries would treat each other politically and economically while respecting human rights.

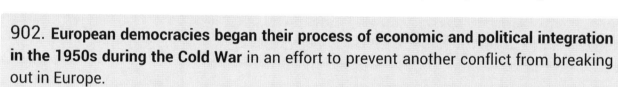

902. **European democracies began their process of economic and political integration in the 1950s during the Cold War** in an effort to prevent another conflict from breaking out in Europe.

903. **Many people escaped communist rule through defections or emigration,** seeking refuge in countries like the United States and Canada.

904. **The Cold War deescalated in 1989 when the Berlin Wall** (a physical divide between East and West Germany) **was torn down.**

905. **Ultimately, the Cold War ended with a victory for democracy and free markets,** as communist regimes eventually collapsed in Europe by the 1990s.

Decolonization
(1945–the 1960s)

This chapter will explore the significant period of decolonization that occurred between 1945 and the 1960s. These fifteen facts will cover some of the countries that achieved independence and what changes were made.

906. **Decolonization is the process of countries gaining independence from being colonies of other,** usually larger and more powerful nations.

907. **The start of decolonization began in 1945 at the end of World War II** when many European nations gave up their colonies as a result of losing power and money during the war.

908. **In 1947, India became an independent nation after centuries under British rule.**

909. **Many African nations gained independence between the mid-1950s and 1975,** with Ghana becoming the first sub-Saharan country to do so in 1957.

910. **Decolonization happened in Oceania, with Papua New Guinea achieving independence from Australia in 1975** and **Samoa** gaining independence from **New Zealand** just one year later.

911. **During decolonization, many countries had to fight for their freedom,** while others obtained it through peaceful negotiations and agreements with former colonial powers.

912. **A particularly violent example of decolonization in Africa is Algeria,** which fought a brutal war against the **French** from 1954 to 1962, leading to the death and displacement of millions of people.

913. **The process of decolonization was often accompanied by civil wars,** as groups within a newly independent nation fought over power or ideologies.

914. **The United Nations played an important role in helping facilitate these new nations'** diplomatic recognition, economic aid, and peacekeeping operations.

915. **In some instances, former colonies were so financially unstable that they had to rely on foreign powers for support,** leading to what is known as "neocolonialism," which is when a country appears independent but still has strong economic ties with its colonizer.

916. **Decolonization led to population displacement** as many people left newly formed nations due to political instability or a lack of resources or employment opportunities.

917. **Decolonization encouraged the idea that all people should be treated equally** regardless of their race or religion, paving the way for **civil rights movements.**

918. **The decolonization of nations led to an increase in international commerce,** as the newly independent states started to establish links with foreign nations that had previously been under colonial rule.

919. **Education initiatives were developed as part of this process, allowing citizens from former colonies to gain access to higher education for the first time.**

920. **During this period, there were significant changes in culture.** For instance, newly formed countries declared other languages as the official language than the one used by their colonizers.

The Prague Spring
[1968]

The Prague Spring of 1968 was a period of mass protest in Czechoslovakia. In this chapter, we will explore fifteen facts about this pivotal event in history.

921. **The Prague Spring was a period of political liberalization and reform in Czechoslovakia** (now the Czech Republic and Slovakia) that lasted from January to August 1968.

922. **It started with reforms led by Alexander Dubcek,** the leader of the Communist Party.

923. **These reforms included more freedom for citizens,** such as relaxed censorship laws, fewer restrictions on travel abroad, and greater economic freedoms.

924. **Thousands of people gathered in Wenceslas Square in Prague** (the capital city) to show their support for Dubcek's efforts and demand greater reforms to be taken by the government.

925. **This was seen as a threat by the USSR. Moscow** saw the Czechoslovakian government as its puppet and did not want liberal reforms.

926. In April 1968, **five communist states—Bulgaria, Hungary, Poland, East Germany, and the Soviet Union—sent troops into Czechoslovakia** to end what they saw as dangerous developments toward democracy.

927. **According to some reports, about 650,000 troops entered Czechoslovakia** in response to the gathered public in April 1968.

928. On August 21st, 1968, **Dubcek announced an agreement that allowed some limited f reform but prohibited the regime's further liberalization.**

929. **This agreement was known as the Prague Spring** because it ended the period of reform and brought back tight communist control.

930. In 1969, **Dubcek was removed from office and replaced by a hardline communist leader who restricted some of his reforms, ending the Prague Spring.**

931. **After the invasion, Czechoslovakian officials pushed for a policy of normalization,** which meant a return to the status quo before the protests.

932. **The Prague Spring was seen as an inspiration to other countries in the Eastern Bloc,** with some of its reforms being adopted by Hungary and Poland.

933. **In 1989, the Velvet Revolution peacefully overthrew the government that had been in power since 1948,** restoring democracy to Czechoslovakia for good this time.

934. To this day, **the Prague Spring remains an important moment of freedom and hope** for those struggling against oppressive regimes.

935. **It became a source of inspiration for many prominent Czech authors, such as Milan Kundera and Vaclav Havel,** who emerged as influential voices against Communist oppression.

The Fall of the Berlin Wall
(1989)

This chapter will explore the remarkable story of the fall of the Berlin Wall in 1989. We'll discover twenty incredible facts about the history of the Berlin Wall and why it was finally removed.

936. **The Berlin Wall was a physical barrier between East and West Germany. It was built in 1961 to separate the two during the Cold War.**

937. After the end of WWII, **Berlin had been divided by the Allies and the Soviet Union** into democratic West Berlin and communist East Berlin.

938. **East Berliners would regularly cross to West Berlin,** where life was much more prosperous and freer compared to the East.

939. **East Germany spread the idea that a democratic capitalist regime was an inferior way to live compared to communism.**

940. After 1961, **crossing to West Berlin without an official permit was not allowed.** East German guards were instructed to shoot anyone who tried to move to the other side.

941. **Many people still tried to cross to the West,** partly to escape the communist rule and partly to smuggle goods to the East.

942. **Around 140 people died trying to cross the Berlin Wall between 1961 and 1989.** It is possible the number was much higher.

943. **East Germans dug tunnels under the wall, hid in vehicles, or disguised themselves as border guards to get past the wall.** Some even used hot air balloons or ziplines to cross the border.

944. **The Berlin Wall stood for twenty-eight years.**

945. On November 9th, 1989, **the East German government unexpectedly announced that citizens could freely travel to the West.** Crowds of East Berliners gathered at the Berlin Wall, and border guards eventually opened the checkpoints.

946. **As news spread of the opening of the Berlin Wall, crowds began to gather on both sides,** armed with hammers, chisels, and other tools to chip away at the concrete barrier. People climbed onto the wall, singing, dancing, and celebrating the end of division and the reunification of Germany.

947. On December 22nd, 1989, **West German Chancellor Helmut Kohl and East German Prime Minister Hans Modrow signed an agreement** to begin dismantling the wall.

948. **The Brandenburg Gate became renowned as a representation of liberation once Germany was reunited;** this historic landmark had been restricted from public access by East German troops since 1961.

949. **In June 1990, after months of negotiations between East and West Germany,** Germany officially reunited into a single nation.

950. **The reunification is now commemorated on October 3rd each year,** with celebrations across Germany, including fireworks displays over the former Berlin Wall site at Potsdamer Platz.

951. **Parts of the Berlin Wall still stand to this day,** serving as a memorial and as a popular tourist destination.

952. **The graffiti painted on either side by protesters has become part of the open-air museum experience.**

953. **In 1963, American President John F. Kennedy visited West Berlin and gave his famous "Ich bin ein Berliner" speech,** in which he addressed the injustice experienced by the inhabitants of Berlin and criticized the USSR and its communist satellites for erecting a physical barrier in the city.

954. **On the thirtieth anniversary of the fall, a light installation was erected on the former Berlin Wall site to commemorate its history.**

955. **Although the reunification of Germany was largely peaceful,** it did take a long time for both sides to adjust economically and politically.

The Yugoslav Wars
(1991–2001)

Explore the devastating conflicts of the Yugoslav Wars. In this chapter, we'll explore fifteen interesting facts about this tumultuous period in history, including how many people lost their lives and how many were forced to flee.

956. **The Yugoslav Wars were a series of wars that happened between 1991 and 2001 in the area known as Yugoslavia,** which is now made up of several countries, including Croatia, Serbia, and Bosnia and Herzegovina, among others.

957. **The ethnic groups that made up the state of Yugoslavia declared their independence in 1991,** and their revolutionary movements eventually turned into full-on conflicts.

958. **The wars were caused mostly due to political reasons stimulated by historic ethnic conflicts over territory** among different peoples living in the region who had their own languages and religions.

959. **Between 140,000 and 250,000 people died from fighting** or related causes like starvation or disease during the war.

960. **Millions of people were forced to leave their homes** because of violence or fear for their safety.

961. **The war between Serbia and Croatia, which lasted from 1991 to 1995,** was especially deadly, resulting in up to thirty thousand casualties.

962. **Bosnia and Herzegovina had a terrible civil war** that took place from 1992 to 1995.

963. **NATO** (the North Atlantic Treaty Organization) **got involved by providing air strikes against Serbian forces** and ground troops for peacekeeping missions during the wars.

964. **The International Criminal Tribunal for the Former Yugoslavia (ICTY) was established in 1993** to bring justice to those who committed serious violations of international humanitarian law during these wars.

965. **To help people affected by the conflict, various UN agencies and NGOs** (non-governmental organizations) **provided medical care, food aid, and other forms of assistance.**

966. **The wars had a huge impact on Yugoslavia's economy;** it lost over $100 billion during this period.

967. **Many cultural monuments were destroyed or damaged during the Yugoslav Wars. Among them was the city of Dubrovnik,** which was heavily damaged during a siege by the Yugoslav People's Army from October 1991 to May 1992.

968. The use of propaganda was common. **Newspapers were used to spread false information about opposing groups,** and leaders tried to influence public opinion through speeches or interviews given to media outlets.

969. **Some countries around Europe closed their borders while others,** like Sweden, offered asylum for those fleeing the war zones.

970. **The Yugoslav Wars are described as the bloodiest conflict in Europe since the end of World War II in 1945,** marked by many war crimes and crimes against humanity, which earned it its infamous reputation.

The European Union
(1951–Present)

For decades, the European Union has been a driving force for peace and progress in Europe. Since its founding, it has grown to become one of today's largest economies. This chapter will explore thirty-five fascinating facts about the EU.

971. **The European Union is a multinational political and economic union of European states,** which emerged throughout the second half of the 20th century.

972. **Belgium, France, Italy, Luxembourg, the Netherlands, and West Germany were the original six countries that began the process of European integration** with the creation of the European Coal and Steel Community in 1951.

973. **Over the next decades, these countries decided to expand their economic and political ties,** creating more shared institutions that benefitted the practice of the rule of law and the development of democratic regimes.

974. **The European countries then decided to unite together into a large supranational political entity to pursue the same goals.** They adopted the name "European Union" in the 1990s.

975. **The organization expanded slowly, with the UK, Ireland, and Denmark joining in 1973 to the European Economic Community (EEC)** – the organization that would be transformed into the European Union in the 1990s.

976. **The number of member states rose to fifteen before the end of the 20th century.**

977. Today, **the EU is composed of twenty-seven member states.** It is likely the number of nation-states will increase in the following years.

978. **Each member country has its own government,** but they work together to make decisions that benefit all members of the EU.

979. **English, French, and German are the most commonly used languages in EU meetings,** although other languages are also used depending on which country hosts them.

980. **The headquarters of the EU is in Brussels, Belgium.** This is where most of the main buildings and offices are located, including their parliament building in the European Quarter of Brussels.

981. Since its creation, **the EU has managed to develop a system of free movement of goods, services, labor, and capital.**

982. **Traveling and doing business between the member states of the EU is very easy,** although there are a few restrictions.

983. **The EU has a common market, and many of its countries use the same currency—the euro—** which was introduced in the early 21st century.

984. In 2004, **ten new countries joined the EU: the Czech Republic, Estonia, Hungary, Latvia, Lithuania, Malta, Poland, Cyprus, Slovenia, and Slovakia.**

985. **Bulgaria and Romania joined the EU in 2007.**

986. **In 2009, Croatia became the twenty-eighth country to join the EU,** opening up further opportunities for trade between its neighboring economies.

987. **In 2016, the British public voted to leave the European Union in a referendum.** This decision was dubbed **"Brexit."**

988. **The EU is involved in almost all aspects of life in Europe,** including trade, travel, tourism, the environment, and justice.

989. **It helps protect people's rights, such as the freedom of speech and the right to privacy,** by introducing laws and policies that apply to all member states.

990. **The EU does not interfere in the national decisions its member states make; rather,** it dictates the general direction of domestic and foreign policy and makes it easier for the member states to engage in economic relations.

991. **The European Union provides financial assistance to member states that are struggling with their economies** or need help with development projects like building roads or schools.

992. **This money comes from taxes paid by citizens within each country,** which are then redistributed amongst other members when needed.

993. Each year, **there has been an official "Europe Day" celebrated on May 9th since 1985.** This date was chosen because it marks the anniversary of when Robert Schuman, a French politician, proposed the idea of a united Europe in 1950.

994. **The EU is involved in many foreign affairs and has international relations with other countries around the world like China and the US.** The EU helps to broker peace deals between conflicting states and provides aid where needed.

995. **It also has its own anthem called "Ode to Joy" by Ludwig van Beethoven,** which was adopted by the member states in 1985.

996. **Every five years, there are national elections for members of the European Parliament** (MEPs). The MEPs represent each country within the EU on issues that affect everyone, such as climate change or security policy reform.

997. **The EU is one of the world's largest economies, with a GDP** (gross domestic product) **of more than $20 trillion in 2019.**

998. **It has its own court of justice called the European Court of Justice,** which deals with legal disputes between member states or individuals within Europe.

999. **The Schengen Area is a zone of European countries that have abolished passports and other types of border control at their mutual borders.** The Schengen Agreement, signed in 1985, has been incorporated into EU law.

1000. **The EU has been presented with many domestic and international challenges,** such as **the migrant crisis in the 2010s** when it had to deal with an influx of an exceptionally large number of migrants from **the Middle East.**

Conclusion

In this book, we have explored European history from the Upper Paleolithic period to the present day. It is remarkable to think of the great leaps and bounds that European civilization has seen in the past forty thousand years.

We have looked at the transition from hunter-gatherer societies to early **civilizations in the Mediterranean,** the emergence of empires, and the development of complex political, economic, and social systems. We have examined how **the Industrial Revolution and the two world wars reshaped Europe and how the Cold War divided the continent for decades.** We have also seen how **the European Union** was formed and the impact it has had on **European politics, economics, and culture**. Finally, we have discussed more recent events, such as **the Yugoslav Wars** and the creation of the EU.

This book has provided an overview of many of the most important events and moments in European history and has shown how these moments have shaped the continent as we know it today. It is clear that **European history is a complex, fascinating, and ever-evolving narrative,** and we can only hope that the future of Europe holds many more exciting stories to tell.

If you enjoyed this book, a review on Amazon would be greatly appreciated because it would mean a lot to hear from you.

To leave a review:

1. Open your camera app.
2. Point your mobile device at the QR code.
3. The review page will appear in your web browser.

Thanks for your support!

Check out another book in the series

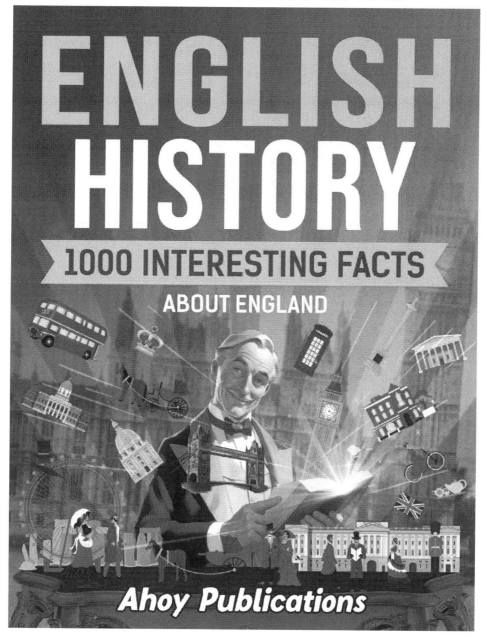

Welcome Aboard, Check Out This Limited-Time Free Bonus!

Ahoy, reader! Welcome to the Ahoy Publications family, and thanks for snagging a copy of this book! Since you've chosen to join us on this journey, we'd like to offer you something special.

Check out the link below for a FREE e-book filled with delightful facts about American History.

But that's not all - you'll also have access to our exclusive email list with even more free e-books and insider knowledge. Well, what are ye waiting for? Click the link below to join and set sail toward exciting adventures in American History.

Access your bonus here: https://ahoypublications.com/

Or, Scan the QR code!

Sources and Additional References

"Upper Paleolithic Period." Britannica, Encyclopedia Britannica, Sept. 2020, www.britannica.com/topic/Upper-Paleolithic-period.

"Neolithic Revolution." Encyclopedia Britannica, July 2020, http://www.britannica.com/event/Neolithic-Revolution.

Hingley, Richard. The Bronze Age: A Social and Economic History. Routledge, 2012.

Cunliffe, Barry. The Ancient Celts. Oxford University Press, 1997.

Cunliffe, Barry W., and Chris Gosden. The Oxford Illustrated History of Prehistoric Europe. Oxford University Press, 2001.

Wright, Rachel. "Minoan and Mycenaean Art." Khan Academy, Khan Academy, www.khanacademy.org/humanities/ancient-art-civilizations/aegean/minoan-mycenaean/a/minoan-and-mycenaean-art.

Rosen, Marc. The Iron Age: An Overview. Facts on File, 2006.

Roberts, J.M. History of the World. Oxford University Press, 1993.

"Roman Republic." Encyclopedia Britannica, Mar. 2018, www.britannica.com/topic/Roman-Republic.

"Greco-Persian Wars." Encyclopedia Britannica, Sept. 2018, https://www.britannica.com/event/Greco-Persian-Wars.

Boak, Arthur E. R. A History of Rome to 565 A.D. Macmillan, 1923.

"Migration Period." Ancient History Encyclopedia, Ancient History Encyclopedia, Aug. 2018, www.ancient.eu/migration_period/.

"The Byzantine Empire." History.com. A&E Television Networks, Apr. 2021.

"The Early Middle Ages." Encyclopedia Britannica, May 2017, www.britannica.com/event/Early-Middle-Ages.

Jensen, Jens Christian. "Vikings." Encyclopedia Britannica, May 2019, www.britannica.com/topic/Viking.

"Vikings." History.com, A&E Television Networks, www.history.com /topics/vikings.

"Charlemagne." Encyclopedia Britannica, Mar. 2020, https://www.britannica.com /biography/Charlemagne.

Hunt, E.D., and Mary Rivier. Medieval Europe: A Short History. McGraw-Hill Education, 2014.

"Art in the Renaissance." Khan Academy. April 15, 2021. https://www.khanacademy.org/humanities/renaissance-reformation/renaissance-europe/a/renaissance-art.

Kort, Michael. The Age of Exploration: Discovering the New World. Rosen, 2013.

"The Scientific Revolution," Encyclopedia Britannica https://www.britannica com/event /Scientific-Revolution.

"The Thirty Years' War." History.com, A&E Television Networks, Aug. 2017, www.history.com/topics/thirty-years-war.

McPhee, Peter. The French Revolution. Routledge, 2017.

"Napoleon Bonaparte." Encyclopedia Britannica, Mar. 2021, www.britannica.com/ biography/Napoleon-Bonaparte.

Smith, David. "Industrial Revolution." Encyclopedia Britannica, Feb. 2020, www.britannica.com/event/Industrial-Revolution.

"Industrial Revolution." History.com, A&E Television Networks, 2009, www.history.com/topics/industrial-revolution.

"Napoleonic Wars." Encyclopedia Britannica, 2020, https://www.britannica.com/ event/Napoleonic-Wars.

"Greek War of Independence." Encyclopedia Britannica, Oct. 2018, www.britannica.com/event/Greek-War-of-Independence.

"The Crimean War." History, A&E Television Networks, 2020, www.history.com/topics/crimean-war.

"German Unification." History.com, A&E Television Networks, 2021, www.history.com/topics/german-unification.

"1848 Revolutions." Encyclopedia Britannica, Feb. 2021, https://www.britannica.com/event/1848-Revolutions.

"Scramble for Africa." History.com, A&E Television Networks, https://www.history.com/topics/africa/scramble-for-africa.

"World War I." History.com, A&E Television Networks, www.history.com/topics/world-war-i/world-war-i-history.

"WWI Casualties and Statistics." History Learning Site, www.historylearningsite.co.uk/world-war-one/world-war-one-casualties-statistics/.

"Soviet Union." Encyclopedia Britannica, June 2021, www.britannica.com/place/Soviet-Union.

"A Brief History of the Russian Revolution." History.com, A&E Television Networks, Aug. 2016, www.history.com/topics/russia/russian-revolution.

"World War II." History.com, A&E Television Networks, https://www.history.com/topics/world-war-ii.

"The Holocaust." United States Holocaust Memorial Museum, https://www.ushmm.org/learn/timeline-of-events/the-holocaust.

"The Cold War." History, A&E Television Networks, www.history.com /topics/cold-war.

"WWII and Decolonization." The History Channel, A&E Television Networks, LLC, https://www.history.com/topics/world-war-ii/wwii-and-decolonization.

"History of the European Union." Europa, European Commission,
    https://europa.eu/european-union/about-eu/history_en.
"The Prague Spring'." Britannica, The Editors of Encyclopedia Britannica,
    www.britannica.com/event/Prague-Spring.
"Yugoslav Wars." Britannica, The Editors of Encyclopedia Britannica, Jan. 2020,
    www.britannica.com/event/Yugoslav-wars.

Made in the USA
Columbia, SC
09 June 2025

59158191R00070